Understanding Money

David Potter

Understanding Money

B. T. Batsford Ltd London

First published 1972
© David Potter 1972

ISBN 0 7134 2163 0

Printed in Great Britain by
Bristol Typesetting Co. Ltd, Barton Manor, Bristol
for the publishers B. T. Batsford Ltd
4 Fitzhardinge Street, London, W1

Contents

Introduction   7

1   Your Money   9
2   Savings   20
3   Banking   34
4   House Purchase and Insurance   51
5   Credit   66
6   Life Assurance   78
7   Stocks and Shares   91
8   The Nation's Budget   105
9   The Council's Budget   117
10 Sensible Shopping   126
11 Running a Car   135
12 Spending for Pleasure   143
Appendix: Useful Contacts   150
Index   155

Introduction

This is a book about money. It covers the various stages from earning to spending as an introduction to money management.

The idea for this book came from a talk to sixth formers about the problems that poverty brings in a material society. I asked them what could be done about it, and one of their suggestions was for more education to help their understanding of money matters. From this remark a course was developed for the sixth formers at Hillcroft School, as part of their minority time syllabus, to cover the many ways in which money affected their lives not only then, but also in the years after they leave school.

In this book the presentation has been revised, based on the experiences of that course. The material can be used with fifth and sixth formers, as part of a non-examination social living course, as a contribution to a C.S.E. Social Studies examination or as a section of a sixth form General Studies theme. I have deliberately avoided any attempt to tailor this book to a formal examination course. It is my belief that the topics covered are too important to be restricted by the content of an external syllabus.

Each section concludes with a series of 'Things to Do'. These are deliberately designed for different sectors of the fifth and sixth year school population. Less able fifth formers will probably concentrate on the variety of practical exercises which encourage and indeed require the student to visit banks, offices and other institutions in order to secure information. At the other end of the spectrum, some of the suggestions call for reasoned essays and discussions. No one reader can be expected to cover even a majority of the exercises. With well over one hundred to choose from, each calling for a considerable expenditure in time, this is no handicap.

I am indebted to the many colleagues who have read sections of this manuscript and offered helpful suggestions. In particular may I single out Mr A. N. Willits whose practical observations on content have been invariably followed and Mrs C. Lovecy who typed the manuscript.

I trust that although this book was designed for a school course, it will not deter readers who have left their full-time education behind them. I believe that the commentaries and facts within are an essential element in the armoury of living.

DAVID POTTER

1971

Chapter One **Your Money**

Money

In the beginning there was no such thing as money. There was nothing to buy. If you wanted to eat you went out and killed for food. Later an exchange system of barter developed. A hunter would keep the skins he had left over; these he would exchange for grain from the farmer who grew crops. What was a surplus for one man or tribe was in demand by another. The difficulty with barter is that you must have something that the other man wants of equal value. Rarely does it work out so conveniently.

What was needed was a medium of exchange. Something of value in its own right which was freely acceptable. The farmer could exchange his grain for this ' medium ' and in time change it again for salt or a horse. This medium of exchange was called money. Some strange objects have taken their place as money. Cattle were commonly used in many parts of the world and still are although they are of little use in payment of small amounts; they cannot be subdivided. Cowrie shells on the Gold Coast in the nineteenth century were valued at 16,000 to the pound which made bills of any size a labour consuming task to settle.

Tens of thousands of different objects have been used as money in various parts of the world at some time in history. Metals have been the most popular and the most lasting, and Great Britain for many years used silver and gold, where the value of the metal was the coin's price. Gold sovereigns and half-sovereigns for spending are no more. The Bank of England used to issue notes for large amounts to make transactions easier to settle, but these notes were always exchangeable for gold on demand. During the First World War, because the

Government had to pay for goods from abroad in gold, it asked everyone for their gold coins and exchanged them into paper notes. For a time the notes could be exchanged back into gold, but as depression loomed, the country went over to paper alone. Today bank notes, and lower value coins which are no longer silver, are accepted at face value: a sign of the confidence that the public have in their money. Some countries have experienced roaring inflation. This occurs when the nation produces more and more money in an attempt to keep the public happy, and there are too few goods to spend this money on. The value of all the paper and coins is greater than the value of goods which can be bought with them. Some countries have experienced tragic inflation. Germany in 1923 and Hungary after the Second World War are examples where millions of notes were needed to buy a loaf of bread.

The old idea of exchange continues today. You have a job, and are paid in money. You are really exchanging your skill and your labour for coin and notes, which you will in turn spend on goods that you need. Except for the few who inherit their wealth, everyone must work to obtain some reward. The uses that they put their earnings to—spending or saving, investing or gambling—will affect their future and their way of life.

It is hardly surprising that one feels rather rich when the first full week's wage packet is opened, or the first monthly salary cheque is cashed. Wages or salaries are both earnings, although the term 'salary' is usually reserved for monthly payments.

With money coming in, income seems more than sufficient for all the expenses with enough left over to spend as one pleases. It is perhaps another story as the 'cost of living' increases and wages stay steady. Management of money is something we should all be good at. We handle money every day, and it is important that we have enough to pay all our bills. If they are left unsettled, perhaps the electricity or gas will be disconnected or we find that a summons for non-payment has been issued in the local court. This is not as far-fetched as it would seem. All too often people get into a real mess when their money will not go round.

The Personal Budget

A budget, or personal sharing out of money resources, is a scheme for planning ahead. Properly produced it will show how much is left over after the essentials of living have been met. Fixed expenses and staple costs, will take most of one's wages. Some of what is left should be put on one side as savings for the future. These savings can include long-term plans for higher priced items such as a car or holiday, and some will be for the unexpected emergency. After this a balance can be worked out between what to spend or save as you please, depending upon the sort of person you are.

Why should a budget be necessary? Why is it that individuals and families find it so hard to manage? In theory the calculations should be fairly simple with bills arriving at regular intervals matching the weekly or monthly instalments of income.

Any system is likely to be upset by a change in job, or a long spell of unemployment or sickness. Even when everything is going smoothly, money handling can be tricky. Wages arrive each week, salaries each month. Bonuses and overtime are extras which cannot be relied upon. Against the regular cycle of income, expenses are out of step. Rent comes round each week, which can be a nuisance if you are paid by the month. Fuel bills, gas and electricity accounts and the council's rate demand come at less frequent intervals. When they arrive, the time allowed for payment is comparatively short. Three to four weeks later, if they are still not paid, a final demand notice will appear through the door. Holidays, once or twice a year will require careful saving in the intervening months. It is impossible to forecast when new suits or shoes will next need to be renewed. An addition to the family will cause the whole budgeting process to be worked out again from the beginning.

Preparing a personal budget is not difficult if it is tackled systematically. The income for a year has to be calculated. This is clear enough if the weekly wage or monthly cheque is always the same. If there is overtime or a bonus to be included, then treat as income only if they are certain. A married couple may have the wife's wages to add on. Private part-time work may also be part of the total earnings.

If you work for someone else, before you receive your wages some deductions will already have been made. A National Insurance contribution, and income tax under the ' pay-as-you-earn ' scheme (P.A.Y.E.) will have been paid. Self-employed workers must buy their own insurance stamp, and keep enough money back to pay the tax bill which will be sent much later. Part-time work is taxable, although often this is left to you to pay.

Everyone needs somewhere to live. Rates, rent, or mortgage instalments must be costed for a full year. Important, but not so immediate, is a small sum put on one side for decorations and repairs. After your housing needs, there is the cost of fuel for heating, lighting and cooking. An all-electric house will have only one bill to settle. More usually there will be accounts coming in from the electricity, gas and coal or oil companies.

Food should perhaps come next. Some of this cost will be the same each week—milk and bread for example. Other items will vary—meat, vegetables and fish change in price according to the season. What will become clear is the average amount spent each week on food, and this can then be changed into an annual figure.

Clothing is always a problem in budget calculations. One does not buy a new pair of socks or a suit every week. It is harder to plan ahead, because most people buy clothes when they are wanted rather than stocking up with articles they might need. Household goods fall into a similar category. Furniture will last for years, and even soft furnishings, curtains and carpets, have a long life. There are the possibilities of buying on hire purchase or through a budget account. These will be considered later. At this stage it is enough that the costs are included.

Services must also be included in the out-goings of a budget covering entertainment, hairdressing, books, newspapers and periodicals, in addition to the television licence. Toilet requisites and cleaning materials are other obvious expenses. In large towns there will be fares to and from work, or in the country the cost of running a car. Insurance for the house, and life assurance policy instalments, savings and pocket money complete the list. If the budget is a practical proposition, income and expenditure should be about the same figure. Ideally they should be identical.

Personal income and expenses

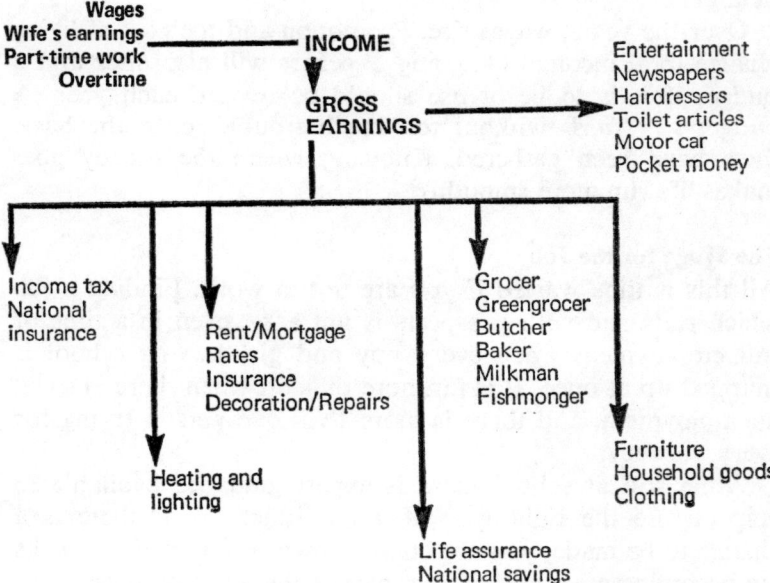

When budgets fail to balance they must be amended. There is not much that can be done about some items. Income will be more or less fixed, unless there are opportunities for overtime. Taxation, and the expenses of living in a house will also be unchanging. Part at least of the food bill will be essential—there may be other more luxurious items where cuts can be made. Overall, it will be savings and pocket-money which are most likely to be altered. Savings are unfashionable with many groups of people, although they are as important to the future as anything else. When budgets fail to balance, cuts should be made in pocket-money spent on unnecessary luxuries. There is nothing wrong with living luxuriously, so long as there is enough money to cover the costs. If not, then this gracious living must wait awhile.

Savings covers a multitude of ways and means—planning to buy a home or car of one's own, or putting something on one side for baby. Planned saving allows for large items of expenditure without upsetting the day-to-day rhythm of a budget. Saving, in the short or long terms, will be covered in detail later.

Over the years, wages rise. Promotion and the cost of living change total income. Outgoing expenses will also alter and a budget if it is to be of use should be revised each year. A budget will work without too much trouble, once the basic facts have been gathered. Knowing where the money goes makes life run more smoothly.

The Wage for the Job

All this is time wasted if you are not in work. Finding a job which suits and with prospects is not easy, even in a time of full employment when every boy and girl leaving school is snapped up at once. It is far more difficult when there is some unemployment, and there is more than one person trying for every vacancy.

While still at school there is expert guidance available to help choose the right type of work. Later on, if there is a change to be made, you are on your own. Examination results are becoming more and more a part of the selection procedure. An employer will want certain passes. Without them, you need not waste his time.

What is a fair rate of pay for a job? In today's society wages seem to vary so much from one firm to another. Earnings often bear little relationship to the importance of the work or even to the qualifications expected.

Some firms pay a very low starting salary, insist on a number of examination passes, and offer a future that includes attendance at evening school and more examinations. Another company demands no such examination results, offers a high starting wage with some overtime, and no further study. Why these differences? Historical reasons play their part. Trade

Unions have fought for attractive rates of pay to offset the uncertainty of unemployment and the dreariness of routine. Those trades which are not organised into unions, and especially shop assistants and office clerical staff, have been left behind in the massive wage race. Employees of national and local government, have always been expected to work for less than they are worth. A more relevant explanation for different wage rates lies in the prospect for promotion and the learning of skills.

Highly paid unskilled, unqualified workers have a weekly wage packet and nothing more. There is a job to be done, important to the community, and many people are satisfied to do it. The future in ten or twenty years time will see little real change in the value of their pay. At the end of forty years service there may be nothing to show for their work except the state pension. There are many for whom the situation is to their liking. They probably get their satisfaction away from work—a contented family life, leisure activities which suit and enrich them, some compensation for the eight hours wasted each day at work.

Ambition does not lie dormant in everyone; it can be a dominant driving force. They want to ' get on ', to make something of their lives, measuring their success by material wealth, even if it consists of a modest house and the latest model car. Routine may be foreign to their nature, and as the job repeats itself they widen the scope of their activities.

Apprentices work hard and become skilled as a step towards the higher position as foreman and beyond; clerks endeavour to extend their responsibilities, looking forward to the day they become section heads and managers. Salesmen develop techniques to increase their orders, and so improve the chances of promotion. For these groups it is experience and the ability to work with others which counts.

Many professions offer a bare minimum wage for beginners. They present a path of promotion and salary increases which come automatically by age or service. Prospects of transfer to higher grades are well known, and readily obtained by the keen and efficient. There is much to be said for half the start-

ing wage of a dead-end job, if after five years the difference
has disappeared, and in ten years one is well ahead.

Working Conditions

Money is important, but money is only one aspect of a job.
Satisfaction at work is relevant too. One third of every working day is spent in the factory or office, and another two hours
can be added for travelling. This is a long time, if work means
boredom. Satisfaction is measured in terms of the people one
works with, conditions at work, and the interest shown by those
in authority. These are factors that can make all the difference
between coming home tired and bad-tempered and arriving
weary but contented.

Prospects are tied to the future of the company. In government service security is certain. In the private enterprise sector
the position is more open. It is wise to ask the company if it
intends to expand or develop new lines. More work will bring
an increase in staff, and promotion is more likely to come from
within. In a declining industry, the management may not be
able to cope, or fails to care, the labour force is static and there
could be a long wait to step into someone else's shoes.

Gone are the days when your salary was all you received.
Now it is but part of the total cost paid out in return for your
services. National insurance contributions are paid by you, and
your employer too; he pays a larger share than you. This compulsory insurance provides safeguards in sickness and in unemployment, in addition to forming a pool for pensions at a
later date.

Other benefits, not in the pay packet, but expensive to your
employer, will come to you much later. A pension forty years
away may seem of little importance but it costs money to
provide, and it makes the transfer from full wages to retirement so much easier. Pension schemes are of two types—
contributory and non-contributory. In the former case you will
find a percentage deducted from your gross wages; in the latter
the firm pays all.

Should you leave the firm some schemes are transferable
and with others you are expected to withdraw all your contri-

butions. A third, middle-of-the-road method allows the pension you have already earned to remain frozen until retirement.

Contributory pensions are financed by a deduction from your wages, the superannuation contribution, and a similar amount from your employer. They are invested with a sound insurance company unless the firm is very big and operates its own pension fund. Pensions are normally based on the average income over the last three years of service. A typical scheme would give one-sixtieth of this average for every year worked, so that someone with forty years service would retire on about two-thirds pay. In addition there is a lump sum equal to three times the annual pension. Pension schemes vary; some provide a widow's pension should a man die before his wife; others allow you to cash in part of your pension in return for a cash sum.

Pensions look to the far-off future. What of more immediate benefits? Everyone who has been at work for more than a few weeks is covered by Social Security allowances when ill or out-of-work. These are allowances to provide a bare minimum, a stop gap until conditions return to normal. Many progressive firms supplement the national scheme with extra money.

Everybody working must be given a contract of employment. It will either list, or tell you where to find the full terms of the contract between you and your employer.

What is the notice that you must give, or should be given should you leave? It can be as little as one hour, or as long as one month—in some cases even more. The longer the period of notice, the greater the stability and security of your job.

Sickness benefit paid by the firm can be useful. Some offer nothing, others one week, while at the other extreme they make up your full pay for as long as a year. An average firm will pay one week's sick pay for every year you have been with them, and perhaps half-pay for a few more months after that. Some firms offer hospital insurance. This makes it possible to enter hospital as a private patient, with all the comfort and service that this implies.

Luncheon vouchers are commonplace today. They may be

worth only a few pence, but they are over and above one's salary, and usually not subject to income tax, making their real worth more than their face value. Holidays with pay vary from two to four weeks or more. Time off for family illnesses and bereavements, study leave for examinations, all add up when fringe benefits are calculated.

Finally there are the perquisites of the job—or the ' perks ' as they are commonly called. Most businesses offer little extras which cannot be translated into money terms, but mount up if they are used. They may be as little as a subsidised social club with games facilities. On the other hand they can be substantial. Airlines offer free or reduced travel around the world to their employees. Bank personnel receive free bank accounts, school teachers long holidays, shop assistants discounts on purchases. These hidden extras make all the difference when balancing a budget.

THINGS TO DO

1 A typical family consists of mother, father and two teenage schoolchildren. The average income is £32 per week. Calculate their income and expenditure for one year. Divide expenditure under the various headings discussed above.

2 How would you revise your budget, if you decided that a new car would be needed in twelve months' time?

3 ' Two can live as cheaply as one.' How true is this remark?

4 ' I've earned my money, so why shouldn't I spend it?' Discuss this remark, and examine some of the choices.

5 Find out all you can about the history of British coinage.

6 Either for your own job, or the job you hope to get, list (a) holidays, (b) sickness scheme benefits, (c) other perquisites.

7 What is the average weekly wage in Great Britain? How does it vary for different types of workers? Discover the difference between wages and earnings.

8 Why do some boys and girls become apprentices when they leave school? Find out all about apprenticeships in different trades. How long do they last, what advantages do they offer, what is the cost, and so on?

9 What are fringe benefits? Discover as much as you can about fringe benefits in different jobs.

10 What in your view would be an ideal job? Would it matter if the surroundings or people were not pleasant? How can you improve your own job by the way you act?

11 How are wages paid? There are many different ways. Keep the list carefully on one side, and see how these different methods are explained at a later stage.

Chapter Two   **Savings**

National Savings Banks

Running the country is expensive. Money is needed for day to day expenses such as Government employees' salaries. Money is also needed to meet capital costs, for example the building of schools and hospitals, roads and airports.

All this is paid for in part by taxation and much of the remainder is borrowed by the Government. Savings with the country, national savings, directly assist the economy. Savings help the individual too, to plan and budget ahead. In so far as you and every other citizen can be persuaded to invest with the nation, in the nation, in its future, the need for income from other sources, and particularly taxes, can be reduced.

One form of national savings is the National Savings Bank. Established as the Post Office Savings Bank in 1861 there are now 20,000 branches, and around 1,800 million pounds on deposit. Twenty million people hold accounts in the bank. It has many advantages. There is strict state security and secrecy. No one can be given any information about your account, and the Government guarantees full repayment of every single penny invested.

Raymond and Violet Carter are twins, and a few years ago Violet decided to go along to her local post office and open an account. She found it was very simple. Violet paid in £5 although the first payment, or deposit, could have been far less. She filled in a very short form which asked for her name, address and signature. A few days later, a brand new bank book arrived through the post. The Post Office does this deliberately, to be quite sure that both name and address are correct.

Violet can now pay money into her account at almost every

Savings schemes

National Savings	National Savings Bank Trustee Savings Bank (and Birmingham Municipal Bank) Savings Certificates Premium Bonds Save-As-You-Earn British Savings Bond Government Stocks Savings Stamps
Commercial Banks	Savings Accounts Deposit Accounts
Building Societies	Deposit Accounts Share Accounts Regular Savings Bonus Savings Save-As-You-Earn Life Assurance
Commercial Savings	Cooperative Societies Finance Companies Local Councils

one of the thousands of post offices throughout the United Kingdom. Withdrawal of money from the account up to a stated yet useful limit may be made at any one of these offices on demand. This is better than the facilities offered by any other savings organisation. Post offices are open for longer hours, including Saturdays, than conventional banks. More hours each week and more offices across the land, means greater convenience.

Against this there are a few limitations. Interest is credited at a very low rate, even though it was increased in 1971 for the first time ever. Also Violet finds that if she makes a number of withdrawals on demand over the counter, her book is retained. The pass book is sent to savings bank headquarters for checking, to eliminate fraud.

Income tax has to be paid on all interest except for the first few pounds. Then again, large sums of money cannot be taken from the account at once. Advance notice has to be made to the savings bank headquarters, and it takes a few days to arrange.

Although the interest rate has recently increased, the National Savings Bank recognises that it is low. These ' Ordinary Accounts ' are not designed for large scale saving and very few people use them for this. Every payment in, and each withdrawal, adds to the expense of administration.

Violet only keeps a small amount in her Ordinary Account today. She read a poster at the post office which explained all about the special scheme which allows every Ordinary Account depositor to open an Investment Account. This offers a very much higher rate of interest. It is not fixed, so that it can rise and fall with the cost of money. To take part in the scheme, Violet found that she had to hold an agreed minimum amount in her Ordinary Account. She did not mind, for in fact it was about the sum she normally kept there for emergencies. She was also told that withdrawal from Investment Accounts cannot be made on demand: one full month's notice must be given. Violet was happy because these were small inconveniences compared with the very high interest yield. She is still at college and pays no income tax, so that all the interest comes to her. Her money is quite safe, with the complete security that is the hallmark of all national savings investments.

The Trustee Savings Bank

Another savings bank is to be seen on many High Streets. This is the Trustee Savings Bank which has an even longer history than the National Savings Bank. The first real attempt to establish a Savings Bank was in 1773 when William Dowdeswell MP introduced a Bill into the House of Commons, although that Bill was defeated. Semi-charitable Parish Banks were set up as early as 1798 (the first by Rev. Joseph Smith near Wendover) and a legal system of control for these banks, later called Trustee Savings Banks, was first secured in 1817.

There are over 1300 Trustee Savings Banks, organised on a regional basis, with the regions independent of each other, although working in close co-operation. They are subject to Government control of their operations, which in turn guarantees the security of the accounts. Their strong selling point is that they offer the quiet atmosphere of a bank instead of their customers having to stand in the same queue as the seekers after stamps, pensions or licences. Ordinary and Special Investment Accounts are offered at interest rates comparable with the National Savings Bank. It is rather easier to withdraw large sums, especially at the office where the account is maintained, and there are deposit and withdrawal facilities throughout the country at other trustee banks.

Customers are offered auxiliary services too. One little used, but potentially useful scheme, is the safe custody service. Deeds, documents and securities for example may be left to be kept in the bank's safe. Unit Trust sales, current accounts with cheque books, and sales of travellers' cheques make their banking operations similar to that of the commercial banks, although on a less wide ranging scale. Eleven million accounts contain £2,500 million pounds in the Trustee Savings Bank system.

Savings Certificates and Premium Bonds

Violet's mother always puts her savings into National Savings Certificates. This was a habit that she began when still at school, and over the years their total value represents a sizeable sum. She calls it her nest egg. First issued in the First World War, National Savings Certificates are an attractive investment for both small and large savers, and they appeal to the Government too. One single payment buys a certificate which is guaranteed to reach a stated value at the end of a specific period. The price it reaches, and the time it takes to get there change from time to time. Their great attraction is that the increase in value is completely free of all kinds of tax, which makes them one of the best kinds of investment for the very rich. Freedom from tax forces the Government to restrict the number of units, or certificates, that can be held. This limit rarely affects the small saver, like Violet's mother, who because she has a part-time job, pays a little tax each week, and so is pleased that the interest on her certificates is tax free.

Over £2,400 million is invested in National Savings Certificates. The Government knows that the great majority of units will be kept for the full period, and this makes the cost of administration low. Early withdrawal of money invested in certificates is always possible, but then the amount of interest earned is considerably reduced.

In 1956 the Premium Bond was introduced. This, the nearest that the Government of the day thought they should come to gambling, retains its face value throughout its life. It pays no interest, and instead an amount equivalent to the interest earned is paid into a pool. From this pool prizes are awarded ranging from £25 up to £5,000 to the lucky holders whose numbers are selected in the monthly draw and in addition there are super-prizes of even greater value.

Winning numbers are selected by ERNIE (Electronic Random Number Indicator Equipment), and it has been proved by the mathematicians that every valid bond has an equal chance of success. All prizes are tax free so once again there is a restriction on the total number of bonds held, but this does not worry Violet's father, who buys a bond or two each month. Bonds are a long term investment, and although they are easily cashed, there is little sense in selling and then buying again. A waiting period of three months before a bond becomes eligible to win a prize, discourages short-term purchasers.

There are over £800 million pounds' worth of premium bonds invested and Violet's father has a few hundred of them. He almost gave up any hope of winning and then in one year he won £25 and then £100. For the last three years it has been quiet again, but he still hopes to see that cheerful envelope containing congratulations and a warrant to turn into cash.

Other National Savings

The National Government is always searching for new ways to encourage more people to save and especially small savers who will make it a habit. One recent excursion into the regular savings field is ' Save-As-You-Earn '. The basic principle is that anyone can stipulate a regular amount to be put aside each month. This may be handed in over the post office counter, be deducted from wages or paid through a bank, including the Trustee Savings Bank or National Giro. At the end of the period, a substantial bonus, free of tax, is added to the total value of the instalments. If this new balance is left undisturbed, a second bonus is paid later on. Restrictions on the total saved each month apply, for this scheme is aimed at the small saver. There is an identical scheme arranged by building societies, and the richer saver can use both.

Another form of savings is to buy British Savings Bonds. These provide a high rate of guaranteed interest over a number of years. Savings Bonds do not go up or down in price. The minimum period they must be held, the comparatively long notice before they may be withdrawn without penalty, and the taxation of interest means that they are not suitable for the average wage earner. They are however, of great value to the man or woman who has retired and is perhaps not liable to Income Tax. The interest is paid, or credited to the savers' bank accounts, at regular intervals, so that they may supplement their pensions.

One straightforward way of saving small amounts pays no interest at all. It is the humble, but useful, national savings stamp. Saving stamps are designed to make saving even easier and although they are really intended to be exchanged for other forms of National Savings, they may be cashed in an emergency.

Big business lends money to the nation and these loans are known as Government stocks. These are still an important method of raising the cash to cover part of the National Debt, and they are dealt with on the grand scale, with daily transactions frequently exceeding a million pounds. Small savers can buy and sell these stocks through the Department of National Savings. A simple form can be obtained at the larger post offices, and this is sent off with a cheque or National Savings bank book, and the chosen stock is bought at the current market rate. This price changes from day to day, as we will see when we look at the Stock Exchange. Only a small commission is charged, and from then on the small man is sharing in the same stocks as the really big firms. These stocks do vary in price, and when it comes time to cash them, no one can forecast what they will fetch. With such stocks only the interest is guaranteed and perhaps the date when they will finally be bought back by the Government.

Saving with a Bank

Probably most people begin to save through National Savings, but there is a veritable army of commercial enterprises, offering similar savings facilities. Many are as safe, and as convenient, as the ones we have already discussed.

Banks have always looked after people's money, and they continue to be pleased to do so. Money is their stock-in-trade—hard cash. Some comes from the balances on current accounts—those that are used in connection with a cheque book—but they also encourage and actively solicit more money.

Deposit accounts are a convenient way of keeping money that is not wanted immediately, but will probably be needed soon. Banks pay a fair rate of interest based on the movements of the bank rate. Bank rate is a percentage, controlled by the Government, which affects practically all borrowing and lending interest rates, both between banks themselves, and with their customers. Deposit accounts are supposed to require a few days notice before you can withdraw your money, but in fact large sums can be taken out immediately.

For the smaller saver the banks offer a Savings Account. This will give a fixed rate of interest, which may be smaller or larger than the deposit account rate, on the first few hundred pounds, and variations in the bank rate are ignored. This does mean that you can work out in advance how much interest your money will earn.

Tax has to be paid on the interest from these bank accounts, which is a disadvantage. It makes them less profitable than other accounts under normal conditions, to anyone who pays Income Tax.

Banks borrow the money in order that they may lend it out again, at a higher rate of interest of course. The difference between the rate they give and the rate they charge, makes up a large part of their profits. Even two per cent adds up when thousands of millions of pounds are involved. Money is lent out to private bank customers, who may wish to buy one expensive item or piece of equipment such as a car or central heating, and to firms who need money to buy more stock, or invest in new plant. Extra goods must be paid for, although they will eventually be sold at a profit, and the firm can then pay the bank back. New plant can well allow a firm to produce more, so making larger profits, and again the bank loan is paid.

Banks also lend out their money to organisations such as local authorities whose income is due at fixed intervals, perhaps only twice each year, but whose expenses, like the weekly wage bill, come round often. In the long run expenses and income are matched, but in the meantime they need to borrow to keep solvent. This is a typical feature of commercial life.

Building Societies

Building societies have grown up to provide a very special service. They lend money to anyone whom they judge is earning enough to repay what he is lent, with interest, so that he may buy a home of his own. The proud new property owner pays back the sum, month by month but first the building society has to find the money to lend. This it does by advertising in newspapers and magazines, and in its office windows. It is mainly the small saver that it wants to attract—people with plenty of money already know the advantages of dealing with a building society.

The actual beginnings of building societies are unknown. Birmingham claims that there were societies there as early as 1775. Those were the days when workers had no social security to fall back on if times were hard. But there were forward-looking men who banded together to help each other, and themselves. They started friendly societies which looked after savings, and helped in time of sickness or death. Other societies were formed to allow them to build houses for themselves. The society would levy a small subscription of a few pence each week. When there was enough in the kitty, land was purchased, and as more money was paid in, building was begun. Those were the days when a building society really did build.

Some of the members would work on the buildings, and as they became ready for use, the order in which members would take over a house was decided by drawing lots. All members would go on paying their subscriptions until everyone was safely housed. Then the society would be terminated.

Permanent building societies, and this phrase is still to be seen in the title of a number of societies, started at about the time of cheap postage, 1840. Investors were invited to subscribe their money, for interest, and it was lent to those who wished to buy their own houses. Representatives came together in 1869 to form the group now known as The Building Societies Association with three hundred odd members.

Money lent on a house is secure. In a time of inflation bricks and mortar become more valuable each year, so that even if the borrower cannot repay, the loan is safe. The house can always be turned back into cash.

In a typical building society money flows into the savings accounts at its branches, and out again as new mortgages, at an ever increasing speed. Repayments of advances and new savings match withdrawals and further property loans.

Building societies at one time offered three distinct types of saving account, and these still make up the backbone of their business. Raymond Carter has always preferred to save with a building society. He chose one with an office close to his home, and he made sure that it was reliable. One simple check is to see if the society is a member of the Building Societies Association. This is proof of respectability itself, but unfortunately there are a few equally good societies which have never bothered to join.

Raymond is a steady saver, and he has a Regular Savings account. This attracts the highest normal rate of interest, maintained for as long as Raymond pays in his monthly instalments. This account is important to Raymond—it has encouraged him to appreciate the savings habit—and it is important to the society too. It can be sure of a regular flow of money, over the years. While other forms of savings increase or decrease, the regular savings accounts total will remain almost undisturbed.

Raymond has a second savings book at his branch. This is known as a Share Account, so named because each saver is a shareholder in the building society, with one share. This gives them a say if they care to go along and vote at the Annual Meeting. The interest rate for a Share Account is just a little less than the Regular Savings Account. Odd amounts can be paid in or taken out whenever it is convenient. There is never any obligation to deposit more money, and it can be taken out without penalty.

There is a third type of account which today is rarely used, known as a Deposit Account. It pays less than the other two types, although operating in much the same way as a Share Account. In theory there is top priority in withdrawing money, before all other savers, but in practice this is unimportant if you have chosen a secure safe society.

Building societies work under several disadvantages. They lend money for very long periods, maybe twenty or thirty years. At the same time they borrow money which is liable to be repaid at short notice. Most branches can arrange a withdrawal of hundreds of pounds almost on demand. Larger sums take only a few days more. The dangers are obvious if

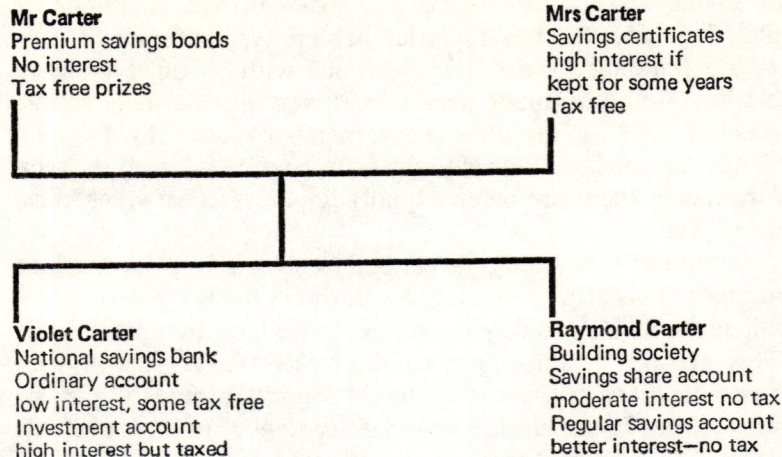

Mr Carter
Premium savings bonds
No interest
Tax free prizes

Mrs Carter
Savings certificates
high interest if
kept for some years
Tax free

Violet Carter
National savings bank
Ordinary account
low interest, some tax free
Investment account
high interest but taxed

Raymond Carter
Building society
Savings share account
moderate interest no tax
Regular savings account
better interest—no tax

more money is taken out than comes in from new savings and mortgage repayments.

One solution is to make sure that the interest rates that they offer are as attractive as other small saving schemes. When there is plenty of money about throughout the country, interest rates go down. When there are credit squeezes and restrictions, rates tend to go up.

Building societies have one special advantage over their competitors. The interest they pay out is free of income tax. What actually happens is that each society pays its tax before the saver receives it and so there is nothing further to pay. Anyone in work, and paying tax is probably better off financially with a building society account; on the other hand for those who pay no tax there are more rewarding places to put one's money as this tax cannot be reclaimed.

Still the search for funds continues, and a number of new schemes have been started by societies to entice the holders of untapped sources of money. A typical scheme will contract that £10, or any other amount, is saved each month for a period of five years. At the end of this time extra interest is added to the account, if nothing has been withdrawn and no instalments have been missed. In the same area are the Save-As-You-Earn schemes which are identical to the National Savings arrangement, and you can take part in both.

Many building societies have linked up with life assurance companies. Because of the tax laws, it usually happens that the amount credited is more than the amount paid out by the saver after his income tax repayment. Such accounts not only show an immediate profit, but they give life assurance cover which is free. This could be important to anyone with a wife and family to think of and provide for. Life assurance is important enough to deserve a section to itself later on.

Commercial Savings

National Savings, banks and building societies account for most of the savings in the country, but not all. There are competitors. In general the higher rate of interest promised, the more difficult it will be to get your money back on demand; you will be expected to wait, sometimes for months.

Cooperative societies encourage their customer members to pay into their share accounts and so provide much needed working capital at a low rate of interest. They depend upon the spirit and ideals of their supporters to supply the cash.

Hire purchase firms and other finance companies can afford to pay high generous rates of interest, but they do not really want small amounts of money. There is just as much work in dealing with a deposit of £10 as £1000. They aim to keep their costs down. Then again they want to be sure that the money is there to be used for a fixed period so they arrange to make it expensive if the money is taken out too soon. They expect and obtain large deposits, and they ask for long notice. They will offer a higher rate if you promise to give one year's notice, rather than just a month or so.

Also interested in money, but not really from the small saver, are the local councils. They never seem to have enough to cover their development projects. Large institutions prefer to lend to councils for they are quite safe to entrust with cash, but on the other hand this can be an expensive way to borrow. So many councils advertise, persuading the medium saver, with a few hundred or thousand pounds, to lend them their money for three, four or five years at a fixed rate of interest. Once the deal is settled neither side can change the interest rate, and the full time must be completed, before the money is available again.

So where should your money go? What advice should you give to someone who has money to invest? It depends so much on personal circumstances—the amount to be saved, when it will be needed, likely emergencies, and the income tax situation. Saving to buy a house should be the number one target of every married couple, and for that matter young people too. Property has proved to be the best bargain in saving over the past twenty-five years.

Small sums of money can be put aside on deposit with a bank, or in a building society. Windfalls and other unexpected large sums, with no immediate purpose in view, should be tucked away for a long term. Council bonds are as safe as can be, guaranteed by the ratepayers in the area. Hire purchase firms' deposit accounts are equally safe, if the company is large and well-known, and preferably is a member of the Finance Houses Association.

Be wise and get proper professional advice from a solicitor, accountant or bank manager, if the sum of money is large or you are in any doubt. Do not be afraid of these professional men. They are well worth consulting, and history, even recent history, is full of examples of money lost because it was placed with unreliable firms.

THINGS TO DO

1 Ask at your local post office for leaflets which describe National Savings Accounts. Compare the two departments, Ordinary and Investment, and calculate the amount of interest that £100 will earn if kept in the bank for a complete year.

2 Find out all you can about the Trustee Savings Bank that serves your area. Compare the savings facilities it offers with the National Savings Bank. Which one would you

choose, and what would be the factors that decide your choice?

3 Ask at your post office for leaflets which describe the current issue of National Savings Certificates. What would £100 worth of certificates be worth at the end of one, two, three and four complete years? What are the difficulties that might affect you if you invested in certificates? What are the advantages of savings certificates?

4 Repeat Question 3 for Premium Bonds. Find out the chances of winning a prize in any month, if you owned £100 worth of bonds.

5 What are the advantages of National Savings compared with private savings schemes? (commercial or your own).

6 Call at any local building society branch and ask them for their balance sheet and investment brochures. Compare the different forms of saving and discover the advantages the society offers savers when they need a mortgage. Are there any forms of savings schemes not mentioned in the chapter?

7 Visit your own, or any other local bank manager and ask him for details of the different forms of saving schemes they offer customers. What are the advantages and disadvantages of saving through a commercial bank?

8 Find out if the local council wishes to borrow money and under what terms. Visit the local council offices and discover how the council finances its short-term and long-term plans.

9 Which forms of saving suit you? How would you change your views if tomorrow you were given £50? What would be the effect of inheriting £2000?

10 List the important factors that must be taken into consideration when you choose a savings medium. What special advice would you give to someone who had been sick and out of work for a long period? What would you advise your grandparents to do if they asked you how they should look after their savings?

B

Chapter Three Banking

Current Accounts

The National Savings Bank, at the Post Office, has more account-holders than any other banking institution in the British Isles. Mention the word 'bank', and most people will think not of savings, but of the familiar buildings prominently positioned on the High Streets of every town and city in the country. Solid, secure looking structures, discreetly labelled with name and business hours.

Banks exist to accept and safeguard money, to arrange money transfers and to lend to suitable customers, commercial and private, whom they are sure will repay. This lending process will be considered later, and it is this aspect, more than any other, which makes the difference between a savings and a commercial bank.

Commercial banks do operate saving schemes, as we have already seen. A savings account for the small saver, and the deposit account paying interest, for larger sums, are encouraged and promoted. It is the current or cheque-book account which is usually associated with banks, and largely because of an aggressive adverting campaign these are now used by more customers than at any time in the past. Much of the mystery and suspicion surrounding cheques has now disappeared.

A cheque is an instruction in writing, addressed to a bank, and signed by the customer, authorising the bank to pay on demand a specified sum of money to a named person or organisation. The usual wording includes the term ' or order ' which permits the receiver to redirect the cheque in turn to yet another account, should he so wish.

A cheque is not legal tender, which means that no one must accept it in payment. In effect most businesses handle them,

Everyday Bank documents

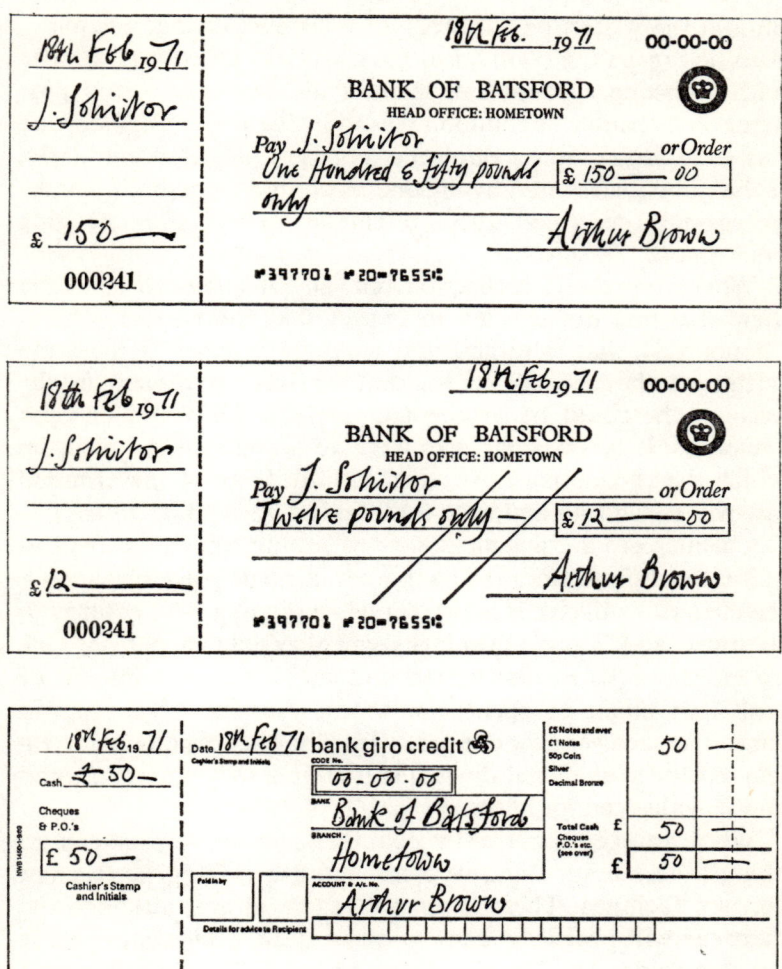

or they would be unable to survive in this commercial world. There are always competitors ready and waiting to offer that extra little service, in exchange for a regular order.

Although not legal tender, a cheque is a legal document. It is a contract, promising to pay a certain sum of money. Should the writer, or ' drawer ' of a cheque, change his mind, then he breaks the contract at his own risk. Of course, anyone with a cheque account can instruct his bankers to stop payment on a cheque. A common reason is that the original cheque has gone astray, and a duplicate has been prepared. Similarly, if the goods purchased by cheque are found to be badly made, or wrongly described, these might be grounds for changing one's mind.

When you receive a cheque from someone, the law takes the view that you are entitled to expect that the cheque will be ' honoured ', that is turned into its value in cash. If then, the writer of the cheque knows that he has no money in the account, he could be prosecuted, perhaps for fraud or false pretences. If he does not even have an account at the bank on which the cheque is drawn, then the full force of the criminal law will swing into action to find him and bring him to trial.

Cheques are a convenient way of settling accounts. Instead of a large, bulky bundle of banknotes, a single piece of paper— the cheque—suffices. It is simpler when sending money through the post, and it has advantages when settling in person. One no longer needs to plan ahead and guess the total amount of cash that might be spent, nor to carry about large sums in cash. The receiver of a cheque is aided too. A cheque is worthless except to the legal owner. It is simple to account for, and and its value cannot be stolen.

Who can open a current account? Basically, anyone can go along to any branch of any bank, and ask to be given current account facilities. There is no need to be of age, although the manager will probably want to know quite a lot about you if you are under 18. The first thing he will ask, is whether you have ever held an account before with that or any other bank. And then he will want the name and address of someone as a reference, who already operates a bank account. There is a great deal of trust and responsibility in receiving a cheque book. It would be possible for someone with no scruples, and fearless of the consequences, to go on an expensive spending spree. It would be short-lived, but even a few days could see cheques totalling hundreds of pounds, not worth the paper they were written on. References will not only be required, they will be taken up. If the name and address you give is some miles away you will have to wait while a reply is received, and if the writer of the reference is himself unknown to the bank manager, this too will be verified. It is simpler to give your parents' or your employer's name as a reference, but if this proves impossible, your bank manager will always find a solution.

Once the formalities are cleared away, you will receive your cheque book. A cheque is a simple document. It includes the name of the bank, and a coded number which identifies the branch. It will probably also include your account number, and your name. Some of this information is repeated in strange looking characters at the foot of the cheque. These are designed to be read automatically and electronically. Today the banks save considerable sums in money and manpower by turning over routine tasks to machines and computers.

Cheques may be either ' open ' or ' crossed '. A crossing is simply two lines across the face of the cheque, and once this is done, cheques are payable only through a bank account. These two lines then provide an extra safeguard, for uncrossed cheques may be presented for cash at the bank where the account is held.

An uncrossed or open cheque is easily converted into the crossed safe version by adding two lines. Crossed cheques are similarly changed by the drawer, who signs across the face, between the two parallel lines. Crossed cheques are more secure, and businesses normally use nothing else. Most private cheques are tendered in payment for goods, rather than for cash across the bank counter; nevertheless, some banks issue open cheque forms to their private customers unless they insist on the crossed variety. Cheques should be dated when they are written. They are useless after six months.

The Workings of an Account

An account has been opened, and a cheque book issued. Where will the money come from to put it in credit? Jack Stevens gets paid weekly by his firm, although not in cash. To cut down the likelihood of their wages clerk being attacked on the way back from the bank, they now pay all their employees by cheque. Jack is a weekly wage-earner, and he takes his cheque around to the bank and pays it into his account at the local branch. He has been given a special book of paying-in slips, which are coded with his account number and the branch code. These slips can be used at any branch of any bank, and once or twice when he received his cheque through the post, he called in at a bank nearer his home.

Linda Clarkson works for the Civil Service, and she is paid monthly. Her salary is credited direct to her own bank, by the Civil Service, who have instructed their own bankers to carry out the procedure automatically. This is a special case of a system anyone can use, if they have a bank account. They instruct their bank to pay each month, or each year, or at any other interval a certain sum of money, direct to the bank account of anyone else. All that is needed is a knowledge of the bank, branch, and perhaps the account number. This facility, known as a Standing Order, is tailor-made for regular payments. Hire purchase instalments, rent or mortgage repayments, come up week after week, or month after month. Annual subscriptions to clubs, payments on insurance policies, and in fact anything which crops up regularly falls within the scope of the standing order service.

Jack sometimes pays money to his account from another branch. This is another of the banks' service, called a credit transfer or bank giro payment. Money handed in at one branch of a bank can be sent to the account of anyone with a bank account anywhere in the country.

Cheques and credit transfers are handled by a large complex system known as the bank clearing. Essentially all cheques on a particular bank are sent to Head Office, for sorting and onward despatch to the drawer's bank. Those for other banks are exchanged at the Banker's Clearing House, and the bankers themselves adjust the difference between the cheques they present and the cheques they receive in return. They have special accounts at the Bank of England for this very purpose. There was a time when an individual could ask to open an account at the Bank of England, but not today. The Bank of England confines its attention to Government departments and other banks, and there remains only a dwindling number of private accounts from the old days.

The clearing operation of a cheque will take a few days. Distant parts of the country are dependent upon the postal services, and many cheques will have to make a long journey up to London, and an equally long journey back again, although in a few places branches have an arrangement to exchange all local cheques. Should the cheque, at the end of the journey, prove to be out of order—perhaps the signature is incorrect, or the date is wrong, or the numerical amount differs from that stated in words—then the cheque must be returned to the branch at which it was paid in. Once these stages have been completed one can be sure that the cheque is in order. For normal accounts a bank will assume that cheques will be met. A business that paid in large quantities of cheques each day, and presented cheques to their value almost immediately, might well have to wait the full period for clearance.

A typical private account will have quite a few transactions each month. Remember Linda, whose pay was credited direct to her account. She has standing orders for life assurance and rent, and usually pays her bigger bills by cheque. In addition she has a small part-time job, typing and duplicating, and receives fees, which usually come in the form of cheques or postal orders. These are paid in every two to three weeks. To keep track of her financial position she has arranged that the bank sends her statements every three months. At her particular bank they are normally sent every six months, but any other period can be arranged, and indeed large firms have them forwarded daily.

Linda checks her statement against her record of cheques

drawn, and counterfoils of paying-in slips. Credits to her
account are explained in some detail, and this includes the
direct credits from her employers. Debits, which are nearly
always cheques, are identified by the final three figures of the
cheque number. Standing orders are either fully described or
a copy of the payment order is enclosed. A statement will
probably not show exactly how much money is in the account.
One reason is that the statement may well have been prepared
a few days earlier so the latest transactions are not included
Another important point to watch, is that some people seem
to take weeks before they get round to paying in cheques.
Unpaid cheques must be deducted from the balance the bank
shows, before a real balance can be found.

One deduction that almost certainly appears from time to
time is the charge the bank makes to operate your account.
This is very puzzling at first, because as most people know,
there is no interest allowed on a normal current account. On
top of that it seems that they want to deduct something too.
Jack Stevens went into this with his bank manager when he
first opened his account. The manager explained that the bank
was looking after his money carefully and safely—branches,
buildings, safes, strong rooms and staff all cost a lot of money.
They have set up an expensive organisation which will speed
his cheques from one end of the country to another, and get
money's worth for all the cheques he pays in. This too must
be paid for. All the expenses and overheads have to be met by
the bank's customers. Most of it falls on those who borrow.
Loaning out the money that is not wanted immediately is
an important source of income. Only a small portion of the
bank's costs falls on the individual current account holder, if
he stays in credit.

Jack's account is operated on special terms which means no
charges at all if a certain amount is kept in credit all the time,
and the number of debits restricted to sixty or so per year.
Because Jack keeps a minimum balance, the bank knows it
can lend that money safely, and the interest meets their costs.

Most private accounts, and businesses too, are charged
according to use. A bank manager will see the number of

transactions, both cheques drawn and amounts paid in, and take into account other services such as the standing order system. The transaction total will be offset by the size of the balance, throughout the six months, and a charge will be assessed. Few banks actually publish their charges, so it is worthwhile calling in on the bank manager to discuss them, either in advance, or later when they appear to be getting out of hand. Students, who must live on their grants and vacation earnings, are usually treated very well. A manager knows that the typical student cannot afford charges. More often than not they will be waived until qualifications and regular earnings arrive.

Banking Services

A bank does not exist solely to provide bank accounts, although many people do not bother with any other services. All the facilities are designed to be helpful, to make monetary transactions simpler when they are needed. One of the more recent is the bankers' card, which guarantees that certain cheques are as good as money.

A banker's guarantee card is an identification card, with account and branch details impressed upon it, and bearing the account holder's signature. When it is presented with a cheque to a shop or cashier, all they have to do is to take a few simple precautions, necessarily checking that the card relates to the same account as the cheque. This cheque is, for all intentional purposes cash and a customer cannot stop payment on a cheque which has been accepted in this way. The bank guarantees payment and the recipient knows this; this is why it was accepted in the first place. This same card permits the withdrawal of cash at any branch of any bank participating in the scheme—in some cases overseas too. The banker's card is an 'open sesame' to instant cash at any time the banks are open, and because of its security many shopkeepers are prepared to cash cheques supported by such a card.

Customers may leave valuables in the safe-keeping of a bank's strongroom or safe. This is not because they are guaranteed to be completely secure—the bank will not accept liability

—but because they do offer substantially more security than the average home. Goods and documents kept at banks must be insured, although normally the premium against loss is much less than if the goods were insured at home. Clients with money to invest in stocks and shares will find that the bank is ready and willing to arrange purchase and sale of stock exchange securities. This is one service which costs nothing—they split the commission with a stockbroker. National Savings can be arranged through a bank too.

Today foreign travel is within everyone's reach. Currency and travellers' cheques can be ordered at any branch, ready for your holiday. Travellers' cheques are cheques guaranteed by the bank or travel agency issuing them. They may be cashed almost anywhere that the law allows. Even if they are issued in Britain in pounds, they will be cashed in the currency of the country you are visiting. To make sure that they are only exchanged by the owner, you are asked to sign them when they are bought and again when they are cashed. The signatures must be identical. The bigger branches have currency of the more popular tourist countries available all the time. Business travellers require more complicated services like the letter of credit, which can be cashed, a portion at a time, all over the world.

Income tax is complicated. An individual with most of his income in the form of earnings as an employee can probably manage without much trouble. A man in business on his own account will need professional advice. If the tax is complicated or just another burden, the bank manager will arrange help. Self-employed customers can often pay the fee the bank makes, out of the tax they save, and still go away happily with a profit. Banks offer an executor service, looking after a deceased person's estate. They take the will, arrange that the legal formalities are observed, turn the estate into cash, and distribute it according to the instructions in the will. In this field they are competitive with each other, although it would seem rather more expensive than employing a solicitor.

The range and extent of services offered is almost unlimited. The established banks are in competition with each other, although there is little to choose in general terms between one name and another. Some services will never worry the small private account—they apply to the big multi-million pound corporations—but there will be the same smile, the same welcome handshake from the manager to everyone, and especially to the new customer.

One bank which is old-established and yet a little different is the Cooperative Bank. It has only a few branches, just one in each of the largest towns, but it is backed by thousands of agencies in retail cooperative stores, where cheques may be cashed and money handed in for credit. Charges are published, and tend to be lower than the household name banks, although the range of specialised services is confined to that single branch in the large towns.

To choose a commercial bank is a difficult task. The bank you select will depend upon the advice of someone who already has an account, and in all likelihood will be one of your personal referees. The branch may be near your home, or where you work. It should be accessible, so that you can call on your manager and obtain his advice when the occasion arises. You can be sure that each bank is aware of the competition, so that they will do their best to see that you are satisfied, rewarding your loyalty with their services.

The National Giro

Despite the impressive catalogue of facilities, the fact remains that most people use their bank simply to hold a cheque book. Transferring money is expensive, and it was with this in mind that the National Giro was inaugurated.

The National Giro is part of the Post Office Corporation and it is a bank. Unusually it is a bank with no branches, but nearly every post office is an agency. It is designed to make the transfer of money, especially between account holders, speedy, simple and cheap.

Before the National Giro opened its doors in 1968 there were many ways of transferring money. Simplest was to put the money in a special envelope and post it by registered post. No account was needed and there was nothing to pay except

for the envelope. Registered envelopes are carefully super-
vised as they travel through the post, and an official signs a
receipt as it completes each stage of its journey. Expensive on
men's time, the registration fee has steadily risen, and still the
Post Office fails to cover the expenses of the service—a simple
way of sending money but very expensive.

An alternative solution is to buy postal orders when the sum
is small, or money orders for the larger amounts. These are
pieces of paper, similar to cheques, sold at their face value with
a 'poundage' or extra charge. This supplement is meant to
cover the cost of printing, and storing the documents in addition
to the administration involved in stocking, selling, redeeming
and checking.

Bank holders have always been able to write cheques.
Holders of Trustee Savings Bank accounts have had the
opportunity to withdraw their money by cheque for a small
additional fee. National Savings Bank, and Building Society
depositors and shareholders could get cheques, perhaps after
a short delay, without charge. What then did the National
Giro offer, that a conventional bank account could not? In the
opinion of the established commercial banking circles it offered
—nothing; from the view of the Post Office—a lot. The Post
Office claimed that it offered the cheapest transfer system available within the United Kingdom, and certainly the most convenient.

Peter Shaw opened a giro account. He went along to his local
post office, and collected an application form and envelope. A
few simple questions which established where he lived, and
details of references, just as with other bank accounts, were
all that were needed. A week or so later he received his initial
supply of the special stationery that is sold at a nominal figure
to all account holders. Peter found that the package was made
up of three main items: girocheques, transfer forms and envelopes.

Girocheques are cheques, with the National Giro as the
bank. They are used to pay anyone who does not hold a
National Giro account, and to withdraw money in cash from
the local post office. The National Giro makes a charge which

National Giro documents

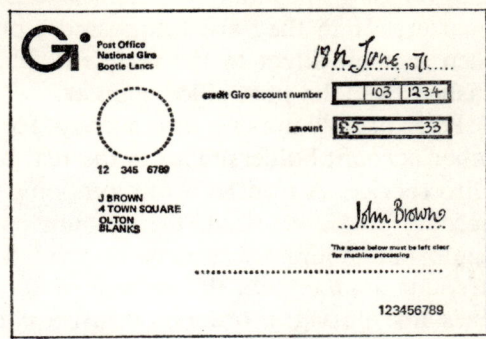

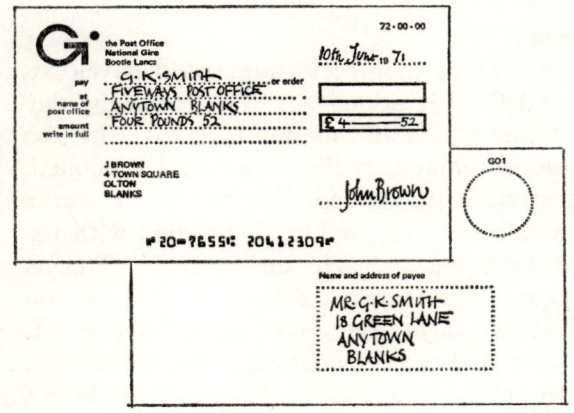

STATEMENT OF ACCOUNT
number   12 345 6789   27 JUNE 71

National Giro
Bootle
Lancs

Summary		
previous balance	20 JUNE 71	£52.16
total debits		49.91
total credits		32.48*
current balance	27 JUNE 71	£34.73

Transactions		£ p
	DEBITS	
25 JAN S 2143211 BLDG SOC		19.37
25 JAN S 1769281 OLT UDC		4.00
27 JAN S 3172962 FPLY INS		5.00
27 JAN P 0016 OUTPAYMENT		10.00
27 JAN T 1031234 B GAS BD		11.50
FEES		4
27 JAN	CREDITS	5.25
D SELF		27.23

J BROWN
4 TOWN SQUARE
OLTON
BLANKS

A Automatic	I Inpayment	T Giro Transfer
Debit Transfer	P Outpayment	for further information
B Deposit	S Standing Order	see overleaf

12 11 123456789 001

is about the same as a commercial bank. Girocheques can be crossed, and handed or posted direct to the payee, or without this crossing they may be sent to the National Giro Headquarters. Here they are 'embossed', or security printed, and then sent on direct to the recipient. In this form they can be cashed over the post office counter.

Peter usually uses his giro account for transferring money to other account holders. This is the real bargain of the National Giro service. A transfer form asks only for the number of the account to be credited, the amount and a signature. Peter's name and address are already printed on it, as is his own account number. On the reverse of the form there are a few lines for messages, orders, or just a cheery greeting.

National Giro Procedure
These forms are sent off in the special addressed envelopes direct to the National Giro Headquarters. The following day the form is received, and all the information is coded. Now the computer takes over. Automatically Peter's account is debited, and the receiver's account is credited. The computer works hard. A special statement is prepared, and matched with the transfer form, and both are put into an envelope. This is sent by first-class post to the recipient who receives it the following morning, just two days after Peter had posted it off. Peter could also have had a statement showing his current balance, although he prefers to wait until six or eight transfers have been made before receiving details. Should money be transferred or paid into his account, then a statement is sent automatically without asking.

How much does Peter pay for these transfers? Almost nothing. The only charge is the printing cost of the transfer form and the envelope and these are purely nominal. How does the Post Office manage? The secret of the Giro transfer is that no money changes hands. One account has £10 less, and another £10 more. The Post Office keeps the £10 under its control all the time, and the balance in the accounts multiplied by the many tens of thousands of accounts, makes a mighty multi-million pounds which is invested. The interest from these investments pays the running costs of giro accounts and Peter pays nothing at all.

Peter collects gramophone records, and always orders them by giro transfer. He cannot find a simpler way of writing for them. It costs far less than any poundage on a postal order or even the postage on a letter. It really is an ultra-cheap transfer system which compares with bank giro credit. Because the transfer slip is forwarded on to the record shop as soon as it is received at headquarters, it takes forty-eight hours in all to get there. Except for the largest firms, few banks will advise holders of a credit immediately it is received, and if they do, bank charges must reflect such service.

A wonderful system. So why does not everyone use it in preference to the older methods of sending money? There is one grave disadvantage. If you want to send money to friends and take advantage of the transfer system, then they must have an account, and you must know their account numbers. Only then will this streamlined system work. The National Giro is new—very new—compared with all the alternatives. People are conservative, suspicious of new-fangled ideas that they do not full understand, and so they do not open accounts. Business firms who should know better are sometimes slow to open accounts, and then when they do they keep the account number a secret. It is this number which is the key to the whole operation.

Money can be paid to non-account holders by means of giro-cheques. If they are crossed, like a cheque, then they must be sent direct to the recipient. An alternative is to send them to be embossed, and then sent on to the recipient who can turn them into cash at the local post office. Unfortunately both these services are expensive, and Peter tries to keep such payments down. They are more costly because these transactions need personal attention, instead of automatic treatment from computer. Nevertheless, the total cost of operating a giro account compares favourably with other schemes, even if many giro-cheques are used.

Money is paid into an account in two distinct ways. For cash, a transfer form, which doubles as a credit paying-in slip, is taken to the post office, and the clerk then send the details onwards so that they can be entered the following working day. Cheques and similar paper documents must be sent with a transfer form direct to the National Giro headquarters. There will then be a short delay, while the cheques are cleared through the normal bank mechanism; once this has been done the usual statement, always prepared when money is put into an account is sent to the account-holder.

You do not have to open a giro account to pay into someone else's account. At the post office an in-payment form can be completed, and the amount of money with a small extra charge is paid over. The handling fee is rather less than you would expect to pay for postage and postal order poundage combined.

Many firms forwarding bills print a giro credit form as part of the statement. For the giro account holder this form can be sent in the usual giro envelope, making the transfer fuss-free and virtually cost-free; otherwise it must be taken to the post office, and it is then treated as an inpayment. Most of these forms are dual purpose with an alternative which permits payment at a bank through the bank giro credit transfer scheme. There is no advantage in using a giro form without an account; it is much cheaper through a commercial bank.

Standing orders can also be paid through giro by completing a simple form of authority. Peter pays his life insurance premiums, and regular monthly payments into a building society savings account this way. Once the form is completed, monthly, yearly or other periodical payments are sent off automatically at no charge whatsoever. This is the giro transfer system working to full efficiency, offering satisfactory service to both payer and payee alike.

Valerie Parsons gets her pay each week paid into giro by her firm. They pay the National Giro a small fee, and Valerie finds that her account costs almost nothing at all to run, because employee accounts of this kind attract special low charges. Like every giro account-holder, Valerie is issued with a National Giro Identity Card, which enables girocheques to be turned into cash at a local selected post office. Large sums still have to be cleared with the headquarters, which is a rather fussier procedure than that used by the banks.

The National Giro scheme is basically a money transfer system, either direct or through the use of cheques. Slowly subsidiary services are being built up. Every customer receives a free magazine, financed entirely by advertising, partly entertaining, partly informative. Travellers cheques may be obtained through the post, and a personal loan scheme through a finance house has been introduced. Overdrawn accounts are not allowed. The personal loan is not cheap, although not much dearer than comparative competitive schemes.

Giro accounts have been operated in many Western Europe countries, uninterrupted even by war, over many years. It is now possible to send money, subject to the laws which control the movement of cash, to many account holders abroad, and they in turn can pay into accounts in the United Kingdom. Other forms of sending money between countries are costly compared with an international giro transfer.

A giro account seems to be becoming more and more an essential feature of living today, in addition to, if not instead of, a bank account. It costs nothing to open, and the charges for the special stationery are modest in the extreme. Transfers between accounts are a bargain in costs that cannot be equalled, and the receipt of regular statements is a typically worthwhile feature that helps everyone to keep track of the way his money goes.

THINGS TO DO

1 List the advantages of payment by cheque.
2 Visit your local bank, and collect a series of leaflets describing the bank's services. Which of the services not covered in this section, do you think you might need?
3 Discuss with friends who use bank accounts the extent to which they use the bank, and the bank charges that are made.
4 A bank lends money to customers who are good risks, for short periods. When would you most likely need to borrow

a large sum of money? What would the bank look for, before allowing you this credit?

5 List the advantages and disadvantages in holding a cheque book as far as you are concerned. What steps could you take to use a bank account wisely and well?

6 Call at your local post office and ask for the leaflet detailing the conditions for opening a giro account. Study this leaflet, and the application form to open an account.

7 Compare the advantages and disadvantages of a giro account compared with a bank account.

8 A National Savings Bank pays interest, and money can be withdrawn on demand without charge. What are the advantages of holding a giro account in addition to such a savings account?

9 What are the main disadvantages of a giro account, when you wish to settle a bill? How can these be overcome?

10 The National Giro Scheme has been described as the bank of the future. Would you agree or disagree with this statement? Justify your answer.

Chapter Four House Purchase and Insurance

Choosing a House

What is the largest single purchase that you will ever make in your life? It will probably be buying your house. Finding the money to pay will affect your budget and your life while you are young and your house will become an important asset in your old age.

This century has seen a move towards home ownership. Paying rent to live in someone else's house is all very well but there is nothing to show for it. A little extra a week as a payment to a building society, and you have your own home. Council houses and flats are quite cheap when the rent is compared to private property. Rents however do seem to increase faster than wages as inflation makes costs rise. Owning one's own home is an attractive ideal. Although it can be expensive, this will soon be offset by the increase in the value of your property.

Few buy their houses outright. Money is borrowed from building societies, insurance companies or the local council. In addition the purchaser will have to meet all the expenses of moving, and probably part of the asking price too.

Jack and Marion have been engaged for three years, and they both have good jobs. They are soon to be married, but they decided from the beginning that they were not going to live in rented rooms or with their parents. Instead they patiently saved with a building society. Six months ago they were busy house hunting.

They live in a large town, in an area with a good choice of estate agents. They soon found that the nicest houses were far and away above their means, and they seriously thought about buying a flat or maisonette.

Buying a house

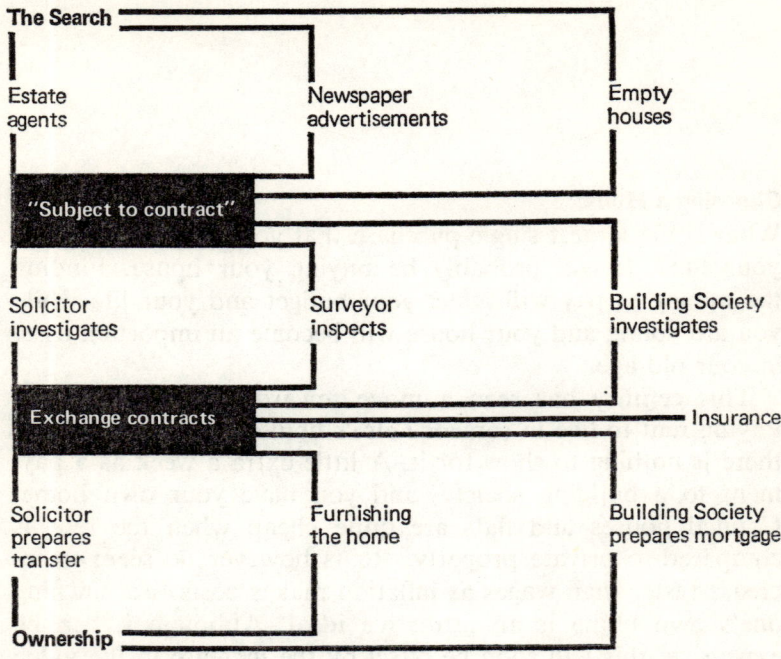

They decided against a flat, because they wanted a house with a garden, and room for their future family. It was a difficult choice, and they soon discovered that a house which they could afford was not going to be easy to find. The language of estate agents is poetic to say the least. Terms such as ' quaint ' could mean hopelessly old-fashioned and out-of-date, while ' compact ' often meant that there was scarcely room to swing the proverbial cat. The estate agent works for the seller, not the buyer. Only when he completes a sale does the original owner pay his commission. He naturally describes the property in glowing terms, pointing out all the best features, and highlighting all improvements. Would-be buyers must discover the faults and the snags for themselves. Jack and Marion soon became familiar with the terms that were used. They came away from the estate agents with descriptions of property within their price range; after discussing the details together they would go back and get an ' order to view '. Sometimes the houses are still occupied and they must arrange to visit when the owner is home; other houses lie empty and a key has to be collected.

Our couple were lucky that they had so many estate agents to choose from, and a wide area in which to live. They quickly decided that they wanted a three bedroom house, not too old, with a garden, not too small, and that there must be a garage. They had done their homework so that they knew how much the house could cost. In this way they could match the agents' descriptions with their own, and only view those that were reasonably similar.

They did not rely completely on estate agents. They also read the local newspaper, although they only bothered to answer advertisements if there was a full description and a telephone number. A few moments talking to the owner saved a lot of wasted time. Now and again they went out in the car, and spotted an empty house that looked just right. They could have called at the rating department in the local council office, and looked up the owner's name and address. Although friends had bought a house at an auction they did not feel that they had enough experience to be happy about buying that way.

At last they found their ideal home. The price was one which they could just afford. Nevertheless they decided to offer £300 less than the asking price, and after some haggling they finally settled at £175 less than the original. They knew that most sellers add something to the price they are really willing to accept. Bargaining for a house can do no harm. The £175 saved came in very useful later on.

Although they had agreed a price, the offer to buy and to sell is always ' subject to contract '. It is no more than a sign of good faith with a small nominal deposit of about £50 paid over to the estate agent, or perhaps the solicitor. Such an offer binds no one; the seller can continue to advertise and to try to find purchasers prepared to pay more and would-be buyers can change their minds and their deposits are returned.

In its simplest form this stage means only that there is a serious buyer and a serious seller.

Checks before Purchase

Three separate steps were then taken by Jack. He called in at his solicitor, to tell him about the property and to instruct him to inspect the legal side—his rights and responsibilities, and to begin the formalities of transfer. He then visited a surveyor, and asked for a report on the soundness of the house. This was not a new house with a guarantee against defects, so it was essential that it was inspected properly. Thirdly Jack called with Marion at the building society where they had been saving for the last three years. There they explained about their hoped-for home, and asked the society to begin the steps which would provide them with a mortgage. A mortgage is a legal process which offers property as a security to the lender of money.

What does a solicitor do? Once he has been instructed by his client, he asks for a draft contract of sale from the seller, or more likely from the seller's solicitor. He then sends out a list of questions. There will be queries as to who is responsible for the boundary walls and fences of the property, because whoever is responsible will have to keep them in a state of good repair. He will want to know about restrictions on the use of the property, and the rights of the owner over neighbouring land.

Leasehold property, so called because all that one buys is a lease or temporary permit to occupy land and the property on it, contains more restrictions than freehold land, which becomes the absolute property of the owner. Leasehold property will be subject to special conditions in the lease which can, as an example, stop the owner from turning the house into a shop, or state the colour of the paint and the type of fence that may be built. Even freehold property is subject to the law of the land and to the bye-laws of the local council.

Payments for the upkeep of the road, plans that have already been made for redevelopment or new roadworks, can affect one's enjoyment of property; in addition they can bring a new owner unexpected and unwelcome expense. These are some of the questions a solicitor will ask the seller, and he will expect satisfactory answers before he advises his client to proceed. Then, as far as the solicitor is concerned the time has come to exchange contracts.

Meanwhile the surveyor has been busy. Jack asked for a full report, because although he expected that the house would be basically sound, he wanted some idea of his likely repair problems, both immediately and over the next few years. Such a full report is more expensive, because it gives the surveyor a lot more work to do, but as Jack had already saved £175 he was able to afford it.

The surveyor gave a detailed report, in writing, on the condition and on the value of the house. In fact the value was very close to the agreed price, but if there had been much difference the report could have been used for further bargaining. The report on the condition of the house covered a commentary on the state of the mortar and timbers, the presence of dry rot and beetle damage, the fittings of doors and window frames, and the soundness of the floorboards. The amenities of the house were mentioned including the presence of the damp proof course (essential as it stops the damp rising from the ground into the house and causing rot), insulation against heat, cold and sound, and when the major items will need replacement. Very important from Jack's point of view was the condition of the drains, and the safety of the electrical fittings. All these points appeared in the report, and although there were one or two items which needed immediate attention, for the most part the condition was very good.

Simultaneously the building society had been busy. One thing it did was to instruct its own surveyor to make an independent report. It was a pity that this survey's contents were confidential to the society, because although it was the basis on which the society advanced money, it was paid for by Jack and Marion.

As it turned out the society placed a value on the house quite close to the purchase price. If they had decided that it would not advance any money or only a small fraction of the total cost, this in itself would have meant that all was not well. In addition to inspecting the house the society had been investigating Jack and Marion's personal affairs. They wanted to know how much they earned and what sort of jobs they held. Some employment means more money year by year, on an increasing scale; other jobs are precarious and are likely to be lost overnight.

Buying on a Mortgage

All was well on each of the three fronts. Formal contracts were then exchanged, and a full deposit of ten per cent of the purchase price was paid. Luckily savings with the building society covered this, although Jack and Marion could probably have borrowed from a bank. From that moment when the contract was signed, Jack and Marion were responsible in law to buy the property whatever happened. There was no backing out. The buyer is always responsible for insurance, because even if the house had been burnt down the next day, the total agreed amount would still have to be handed over. Only a serious irregularity, which the seller knew about all the time, but had not mentioned to the buyer, could cause the contract to be cancelled.

The solicitor continued his investigations, inspecting the deeds and the land registry entry. This is the legal evidence of the seller's right to the property. They do not necessarily mean that the seller has the right to sell, because he may have bought the house on a mortgage. The mortgagor's consent is also needed.

It is essential to agree on the completion date. This is when the keys will be handed over, and the seller must leave the house empty. It is not an easy day to fix, for usually when one person sells, he is buying another property and he will want the date for both houses to be the same. In this way a long chain of buyers and sellers can be built up, all moving on the same day.

The solicitor arranges with the building society, so that the purchase price will be ready, checks the mortgage deed is fair and correct, informs the land registry of the transfer, pays any stamp duty due, and finally hands over the purchase price in exchange for the deeds and keys. More often than not the deeds are taken over immediately by the building society, as security for the money it has advanced. At least Marion and Jack now own a house of their own. They will be repaying the amount they have borrowed over the next twenty-five years.

Building societies exist to make home ownership possible. In times when money is scarce, the amount they have to lend will be limited. It is crucial that would-be house owners should begin the search for a society that is prepared to help as early as possible. Regular savers and shareholders with a building society will get more consideration and probably some priority compared with the casual caller.

It is usually necessary to withdraw nearly all one's savings to meet the cost of a home. Some of the expenses have already been noted—solicitors' and surveyors' fees and the deposit on the house. A building society advances a fixed percentage of its valuation of the property. Take a selling price of £5500 where the building society thinks the market value is £5000, then if it is prepared to lend 90 per cent, this will only be £4500. The difference of £1000 has to be found as the deposit, and this can be too much. Bargaining and bringing the selling price down by only £250 to £5250, would reduce the deposit by a quarter.

Direct expenses are only the beginning. Furniture removals, new furniture and furnishings, rates and possibly ground rent, insurance and fuel are all part of the expenditure which must be expected from the moment the contract is signed.

Sometimes it is hard to find a building society prepared to advance money. There are two other main sources worth exploring. Many councils will advance money if the house or flat is to be occupied by the borrower. They follow a similar routine to the building societies. Some life assurance policies carry the important and valuable right to cash for home purchase, and this is yet again a mortgage advance in disguise.

The total costs of house purchase vary so much. They depend upon the price of the house, the size of the mortgage, the difficulties noted by the surveyor, the rate of government duty payable on higher priced properties, in addition to the land Registry charges. On a £5000 home the total cost, including removals, but ignoring new furniture will be somewhere in the region of 5 to 10 per cent of the £5000.

Mortgage repayments are fixed when the contract is signed, and they are based on current rates of interest. There will be a section in the contract which allows the lender to change this interest rate, by giving notice. In such an event the amount paid each month could rise, or fall, but in practice as long as sufficient has been repaid to reduce the original loan, most lenders are prepared to keep the monthly instalments pegged. Mortgage repayments receive tax reliefs. Anyone who pays the normal income tax rate, will find that if they tell their tax office, they will be a little better off each pay day.

In the early years of repayment, most of the monthly instalment is made up of interest. After ten years of a twenty-five year loan, less than one quarter of the amount borrowed will have been repaid. As the years progress, each succeeding instalment contains less and less interest, and the capital is paid off more quickly. In any event, the value of the house will have increased.

A home is an investment; a home of one's own offers far more security than rented houses or rooms. Property can be developed and decorated to suit oneself, with the knowledge that this all adds to the value. When the time comes to sell, the asking price reflects the improvements that have been made over the years.

Northern Ireland and Scotland

The stages in buying a house in England and Wales have been described. There are a few variations in the law and practice within Northern Ireland and Scotland.

In Northern Ireland property is practically all leasehold; many of the houses are part of a lease contract of 999 years or even longer. Estate Agents charge their fees to the buyer, not to the seller. This is an arrangement first started during the Second World War when houses were very scarce, and sellers became unwilling to pay the agents' commissions.

In Scotland most property is of 'feudal' tenure. In practical terms this is the equivalent of holding it on a perpetual lease. Leasehold property throughout the United Kingdom is subject to an annual rent, often known as ground rent, which is paid to the holder of the freehold. In Scotland, in place of ground rent, a 'feu duty' become payable to the Superior, as the landlord is termed. Although estate agents are to be found in Scotland, the buying and selling of houses is conducted mainly by solicitors. When this happens, the solicitors will charge a commission for acting as a 'property agent'.

There is no informal stage in the buying of a house in Scotland similar to the time when a would-be purchaser makes his offer 'subject to contract'. The buyer makes a formal offer at a stated price, subject to a number of conditions which include such points as proof of ownership, date of occupation and so on. If the seller accepts this offer then it is binding on both parties. Mortgages are also unknown in Scotland. Instead the property is transferred immediately into the name of the building society, on terms similar to an English mortgage. When the payments have been completed the society agrees to reconvey or transfer the house to the buyer.

Home Insurance

From the moment that the contract is signed to purchase a house, it must be covered by insurance. This is not a legal requirement but a commonsense precaution.

Every time we insure against the worst happening, we are gambling. Insurance is a bet that something may happen. With luck, disaster does not strike, the bet is lost, and everyone is happy. This is one bet that we hope we never win. Should there be trouble, then the insurance policy comes into its own. There will be little or no financial loss, although there may be inconvenience.

A basic principle of insurance is that no one should make a profit from it. The amount insured, the cover, should be enough, and just enough, to replace what has been lost. The document, a contract between you and the insurance company, which details exactly what is involved, is called a policy. At

one time there was a tendency to call certain policies comprehensive. Unlike a comprehensive school, which admits all-
comers, comprehensive insurance policies did not cover every
form of loss. They contained only some of the possible ways
in which damage might be suffered. Modern policies admit to
this selection of risks, and the old description is being dropped.

Home owners require to cover the value of buildings, and
contents against loss. Families living in rented accommodation
will probably be well served by contents insurance alone.
Policies vary; it always pays to shop around, looking at the
offers of three or four firms at least. Brochures, with their
suggested cover are not legal documents, and they are not
binding. Although there may be some difficulty it is well worth
insisting that you are given a copy of the policy, which alone
states just what the company is prepared to insure.

Once satisfied, you will be asked to complete a proposal
form, which asks for personal and other relevant details. On
this form will appear a description of what you wish to insure,
and how much it is worth. It is fundamental that the company
knows if the house is built of brick and stone, or for instance,
of timber throughout. This will certainly affect the amount they
charge you, as will your past record with insurance companies.
If you have made a habit of losing watches or jewellery, then
they will not want to insure these unless there is an extra
charge. The amount due as premium is in most cases payable
each year in advance.

A typical modern home insurance policy is a complicated
contract; it must be if both the insurance company and the
client are to know exactly what it means. Small type, the bane
of old time policies, is on its way out. The meaning is clear
enough these days if the sentences are taken phrase by phrase.

'Buildings' does not mean that just the house is covered.
Outbuildings such as the garden shed and greenhouse are
also part of the home. An ordinary policy expects your home
to be used for domestic purposes only. Use the garage to repair
your friends' cars, charge them for your skill, and the garage
will no longer be insured—at least by this particular policy.
This is the time when you would like to vary the terms of a

standard policy. It can be done by an endorsement which alters the contract. Endorsements add or take away cover. If the alterations are complicated the insurer may well suggest a separate policy.

Loss or damage to buildings will be covered if caused by fire, lightning, earthquake, aircraft, riots, strikes, malicious persons, theft, storm or flood, to name but a few. There is little point in cataloguing the long list of possibilities; there are exceptions even here. It is a brave insurance company that is prepared to offer riot protection in Northern Ireland. They have seen too many disturbances to want to take on that risk.

The more likely the event happening, the larger the premium an insurance company will charge. Premiums on household policies are very very small because each disaster taken separately is equally remote. Insurance is designed to meet the unexpected and uncertain, which could be crippling financially if it occurred.

It is not only the actual loss and damage to a building which is covered. If a house is gutted by fire, then presumably the owners will want to restore it to good condition again. Architects, surveyors and solicitors will be needed, and their fees are covered by the policy.

It is often overlooked that a policy will cover exactly what it states; this is why they are so long-winded, describing so many different ways in which damage can be sustained. To see what is covered, borrow the policy that covers your own home.

In addition to protecting the buildings there are also the contents to be considered. Contents, especially in this crime-prone age, need to be insured by everyone. It is far cheaper that one would think, and the sight of possessions scattered around after a break-in or charred and almost unrecognisable following a fire, brings this lesson home as nothing else can. Insurance does not bring the original property back—but it goes a long way to relieving the financial worry.

Content insurance is separate from the building cover. All the contents are included with perhaps the exception of deeds, stamps, coins and the like, and maybe motor vehicles and accessories which have their own separate insurance.

Contents are insured against the same hazards as the buildings. Some policies are far more generous and do not even demand that the contents be within the building at the time of loss. Perhaps you take your coat to work each day and leave it in a locker or cloakroom. One day it is stolen—then it will be paid for under your home contents policy. You are travelling along when a bus or train catches fire, and your clothes or suitcase are singed. Once again your own home policy covers you against loss. Should you decide to change houses, then your property is fully protected for mainland removals; it will need an endorsement if your goods go outside the United Kingdom or across the sea.

Additional risks which the insurance company takes on are becoming more and more a feature of the new competitive policies. These so-called fringe benefits make some policies at first sight more expensive but are a bargain when taken as part of a package deal. So if the house burns down, blows up, or is engulfed in flood water; where do you live? With friends of you are lucky; otherwise in a hotel. Your rent or bill will be paid by the company. An accident to you or a member of your family, could result in a cheque from the firm, if the accident had been caused by anything that was insurable under the policy.

Personal liability has always been a very cheap insurance—£1 covers £100,000 or more. This is the legal liability you have towards others should you cause them damage or loss of any kind, however accidental. Accidents are a perfect defence to criminal charges, but they are no defence in civil cases. Damage caused must be paid for, and the papers and courts are full of heavy awards of damages paid to young and old alike.

Jogging along in a day-dream, with umbrella swinging high, you accidentally poke the tip into someone's eye. Very unlikely indeed, which is why personal liability insurance is so cheap, but it can happen. A civil claim is started against you; should the victim depend upon that eye for his livelihood, then costs and damages together could amount to far more than you have ever thought about. Personal liability insurance give you full legal representation in court, and the company foots the bill for damages, up to the policy's limit, should you lose. Such a cheap form of insurance cannot be overlooked if it forms part of a package deal.

Other Types of Insurance
Remember that policies, and especially package policies vary from company to company. If you have a policy already, then study it well; if you are thinking of insuring then get three or four different companies' propositions. Similar schemes exist for motor vehicles, and the package policies offer good value compared with the slightly cheaper so-called comprehensive cover.

There are two ways of obtaining insurance. You can call in at an office, or answer an advertisement. You will almost certainly only be shown the policies of a particular company. A better scheme is to visit an insurance broker; he is a very useful person to know. When professionally qualified (and all too often part-time agents set themselves up as brokers when they are nothing of the sort) he will have expert knowledge of the insurance world and he will be able to offer sound advice. Naturally enough he will want to know what is to be insured, and he will probably mention a number of risks that you had never thought about. He will obtain proposal forms from different companies, for you to make the final choice. Normally there is no charge for his services—he is paid by the insurance company, receiving a percentage of the premium paid.

It is possible to insure anything in which you have an interest—all you must do is to show that you will suffer financial loss if catastrophe strikes. Only your loss will be met—it is a fundamental principle of insurance that you cannot make a profit. A famous pianist can insure his hands, a celebrated singer her voice, but unless you can show that you too will lose money if there is damage, it is not possible to insure against someone else's bad luck.

When you go on holiday, you can insure against all the problems that could happen—loss of baggage, forfeiture of deposit in case of illness, and even bad weather. The argument is that rain could affect your enjoyment of the holiday, so if more than a certain stated amount falls during the day between 10 am and 6 pm then you are entitled to recompense. It is hardly surprising that within the British Isles, the premiums for weather insurance are on the high side.

Protection sums up the whole idea of insurance. It is an umbrella, keeping the worst of bad fortune off you, or at least reducing it to a manageable level. Life insurance will be covered later, but there are many other possibilities. Every time you post a registered letter, part of the fee is an insurance premium against loss. Holiday package tour operators and school journey organisers usually require an insurance fee, or alternatively include it with the other expenses. The planners of an open air show make sure that damage by gales, or cancellation through rain, does not affect the total takings, by taking out insurance cover.

Only the very largest organisations can afford to ignore cover altogether. Local authorities will have buildings and equipment scattered around their area. Disaster, if it strikes, will hardly strike in more than one or two places at once. A fire in one building will not affect another half a mile away. Losses there will be, but over a year or two they will average out to a level equal to, or probably less than the premiums an insurance company would have asked for. If they are doing their business correctly premiums must amount to the average losses, with a little extra besides for profit.

The home owner, the individual with his car or his shop, cannot afford and should not even dream of a life without the protection and strength of the insurance companies.

THINGS TO DO

1 Examine the estate agents' windows in our neighbourhood to get some idea of the level of prices being asked for property. Assume that you want to buy a flat or house. Write down the facilities you would expect, and then discover the probable price you would have to pay. What difference does the area make to the price asked?

2 What is the difference between leasehold and freehold? Which of these is more advantageous—for a house owner and for a flat dweller?

3 Mortgage repayments each month are normally restricted to an amount equal to the borrower's weekly wage. Looking ahead, what wage will you have to earn to be able to afford the type of house that you want? How could you manage to buy such a house before you are earning so much?

4 Look up, in your library for example, the total costs that you can expect to pay on a house costing £5000, with a 90 per cent mortgage. Include the average solicitor's and surveyor's fees. If the library cannot help you with these figures, ask them where this information can be found, and search it out for yourself.

5 Discuss the advantages and disadvantages of buying a house compared with living in a council house of the same size, in the same area.

6 Visit your local insurance broker or insurance company and ask them for full details of home insurance. Take away and study the proposal form and brochure. List any problems which occur to you, and which you would wish to have cleared up before taking out an insurance policy.

7 Obtain a copy of a home insurance policy. There should be one in your home. Look at the items covered, and check on the exceptions. What risks are usually excluded?

8 List five or six different areas or items in which you are, or are likely to be, involved and which would need insurance.

9 Find out as much as you can about insuring against bad weather, both personal policies for holidays and day policies for outdoor events.

10 Insurance is a gamble. Discuss this remark, and list the points in favour and against such 'gambling'. How does insurance differ from real gambling?

Chapter Five Credit

Living on Credit

Each morning the paper and milk are delivered to our homes. We do not pay for them each day as they arrive, but wait until the end of the week. In the meantime we have been living on 'credit'—that is using goods before we pay for them. So it is with gas, electricity and the telephone. We use these services and settle the bills at a later date. Perhaps you did not think you were living on credit when you switched on the light, or made a telephone call. There is no other way of paying for these services. One thing they all have in common. There is no extra charge for credit.

The world is full of goods which we would like to buy, but cannot afford. We could wait until we had saved up the purchase price. Modern life has found another method—credit. It is not always possible for people to wait. For example a newly married couple, savings exhausted buying their home, are unlikely to take kindly to the idea of patience while they save even more. They will want furniture right away. Possibly a new job calls for a difficult cross-country journey. A car will not be a luxury, but essential.

BUYING MONEY	
Hire Purchase	**Monthly Accounts**
Credit Sales	**Credit Cards**
Overdrafts	**Hiring**
Personal Loans	**Finance Houses**
Budget Accounts	**Money Lenders**
Trading Checks	**Pawnbrokers**
Home Shopping	

We are all consumers buying goods and services. The business world knows the need for credit and supplies it; their methods are the different ways of borrowing money. Such facilities are offered, either to make money for the organisation providing the credit, or to improve trade in the firm offering it. Borrowing money is expensive, and you, the consumer, may have to pay for it. It can be justified if the purchases are essential, but not for unnecessary luxuries.

Hire Purchase

'Hire purchase' is a common form of credit. For a lump sum down, 'the deposit', and a promise to pay a fixed amount, 'the instalment', each month, the goods will eventually belong to the buyer. It is normally used for items in the middle price range: motor cars, motor cycles or television sets. A form is prepared stating the cash price, deposit, number of instalments, how often they are due, and the amount of each one. From these figures the actual extra charge for credit can be worked out.

Ignore all interest rates that may be quoted by the salesman. Percentages are easy figures to twist and turn. Look at the cash price, then add the deposit required and all instalments. This total will give you the difference between cash and hire purchase prices. This difference is the credit charge. A car with a cash price of £500, may be offered for only £100 deposit. If the instalments amount to £18.75 each month for two years, the total hire purchase price will be £550. But remember you only borrowed £400, because you paid £100 as a deposit. From the moment of the first instalment you have paid something off the loan, and on average you have borrowed £200 for two years. The true interest rate works out at about $12\frac{1}{2}$ per cent per year. These figures are only an example; the real rate could be much higher.

Why so expensive? In the first place the garage that arranges the hire purchase contract will collect a commission from the finance company, included as part of the repayments. Monthly payments are sent in, and the company has to employ staff to check them, keep records, remind purchasers who are behind with their payments, or send investigators to trace vehicles. All such expenses have to be covered. People may even disappear. Unfortunately, the careful and honest must carry the less scrupulous buyers, and these hazards must be allowed for in the repayment figures.

Hire purchase is an accepted feature of life today. The goods bought under such a contract remain the property of the seller until all the instalments have been paid. You, with your car, are legally considered to be hiring it for two years. The last instalment includes a nominal penny or two which changes the contract from a hiring to an outright purchase. There were many abuses in the past. Today when a certain amount has been paid, the goods cannot be taken back without a court order. The buyer and the lender both have their rights.

Public utilities such as the electricity and gas boards lead the way in persuading consumers to live on credit. So cookers, fires and refrigerators are regularly sold in this manner. Oil and other types of central heating units are offered with easy credit terms. Even holidays, with a ' go now, pay later ' slogan can be arranged.

Buying Money

A similar scheme to hire purchase is the credit sale. The technical difference between the two methods is that from the moment the deposit on a credit sale is accepted, the purchaser owns the articles absolutely. There is no question of the goods being on hire. Credit sales are often arranged by stores, and in some cases the fees are a little lower. A typical rate is 5 per cent added on to the cash price; if the bill is settled in nine equal monthly instalments a true interest rate of over 13 per cent per year. Sometimes a deposit is asked for but usually payment is by instalments only.

In all these schemes, the customer is buying money. Perhaps hiring money for an agreed number of months would be a better description. Banks make their livelihood lending money. If you can get it the cheapest regular form of finance is likely to be an overdraft. This is an arrangement with the bank, to write cheques for a certain sum over and above the balance in the account. The overdrawn balance is charged interest on a day-to-day basis, which varies with bank rate. Unfortunately, for the private customer, overdrafts are becoming a thing of the past.

Today they are being replaced by personal loans. These are similar, but cost more. Usually the sum loaned must be repaid at regularly monthly intervals, and a credit charge is added to the original sum. The figure quoted will seem to be quite reasonable. Because it is added to the initial loan, and the sum outstanding is reduced each month, the true interest figure is about twice the quotation.

An overdraft can theoretically be called in at a moment's notice, while the terms and periods of personal loans are fixed. Personal loan side benefits include insurance, postponing payments in case of sickness and cancelling the balance outstanding if the borrower dies. Overdrafts are only permitted when there is some sort of security; the deeds of a house, stock and share certificates or a life assurance policy are usually deposited with the bank. Securities are less often asked for with a personal loan especially from people with good jobs, and a regular income. There is some truth in the saying that only those who have money find it easy to borrow.

There are two popular forms of credit offered by retail stores. Large department stores, and some multiple-firms with many branches, offer a 'budget account' with 'revolving credit'. You agree to pay a fixed amount each month. Before you open the account you will be asked to visit the store and, as with all credit schemes, fill in a form that asks for personal particulars. When they have been checked and cleared, you are offered a credit, equal to say eight times your monthly payment. If you decide that your instalment will be £5 each month, then you will be entitled to take goods totalling £40. Imagine that you do this in April. You owe the firm £40, which is reduced to £35 in May and £30 in June. Your credit limit is still £40, so you could, if you wished, buy £10 worth of goods more in June, bringing the amount owed back to £40 again. All the bills, and payments need a large staff to keep track of them. To help pay their wages most firms charge a small fee, about one per cent on the balance outstanding each month. Taking our example this cost 40p in April and 35p in May.

These accounts do tend to encourage some people to live beyond their means. There is always the cushion of £40 worth of goods more than they can afford. Never ending, as part is paid off, by the revolving credit idea, more goods are bought.

Small firms are not able to offer the same facilities. One solution is the trading check. Checks are bought from an organisation, £10 worth perhaps costing £10.50, and they are paid back over 21 weeks at 50p each week. As an alternative checks are written out as they are needed for the exact amount of the goods. In many cases a representative will call at the house each week for the balance due, making the trading check system simple to use.

These checks cannot be spent at any shop—only at those which display the check trader's sign, or which appear in the directory issued with the checks. In most cases these shops will charge as much, if not more than their competitors. They will certainly not sell for less, because although participation brings them extra business, traders turn the checks into cash at a discount of anything up to 10 per cent. For every £10 spent, they may be paid only £9 in cash.

This is the continuing problem with all credit systems. Unless you are actually lent money, you will be restricted to places which recognise your account, or trading checks.

Credit without Charge

A popular form of credit trading in disguise is the home shopping club. An organiser will act as representative for a large mail order firm. She will visit families in their homes, with a copy of the company's catalogue—a large colourful book listing all the goods for sale. The biggest firms offer practically everything that a family could possibly need or want, from clothing to car accessories, and from paint to Christmas hampers. The organiser takes orders, and accepts the payment by instalments over 12, 20 or 38 weeks. For her trouble she receives a commission usually from 10 to 12½ per cent. Most catalogues make the point that there is no extra charge for this credit—it is worth checking that the prices have not been increased in the first place above those in the shops and, what amounts to the same thing, that there is no discount for cash. Rarely do these firms run sales with reductions off their published prices. Normally it will be cheaper to shop around, but part of the attraction of these clubs is the weekly visit of the organiser, and the chance to choose goods in the peace and quiet of one's own home.

In addition to the revolving credit budget accounts, most large department stores make a point of offering credit without charge. This generosity is confined to a 'monthly account', where all the purchases are totalled together, one bill forwarded at the end of the month, to be paid in turn by a single cheque. Why should they bother to go to so much trouble? Cash transactions cause little paperwork and the money is in the till; credit accounts need staff to make out the bills, enter them into ledgers, despatch accounts, and chase outstanding debts. The store has to wait for its money. Even if it replaces most of the staff by a computer, costs remain high.

Partly the reason lies in history. Small traders in neighbourhoods with moneyed customers found that to attract business they had to be prepared to grant credit. Sometimes this seemed to go on for ever—not paying one's tailor was fashionable years ago. Towards the end of the nineteenth century, the growth of the large store forced these newcomers to adopt a similar system if they were to compete with their long established rivals. It was not so important if the customer was slow in paying. Staff and money were cheaper then.

Successful firms find that they need more and more staff and machinery simply to handle account customers' paper work. All this is expensive, yet who pays? Not the account customer, because normally nothing is added on to monthly accounts when they are settled promptly. Because overheads, that is the expenses a firm must foot to make a sale, are increased, indirectly everybody pays. Either the retail price must be raised, or discounts rarely given. Not all account overheads are a dead loss. Some sales would never be made if customers could not buy on credit. The staff and building are already there, so such extra sales mean added profit. Increased turn-over encourages efficiency—offsetting account costs.

Small firms have often cast envious eyes on their depart-mental store competitors who were able to offer apparently unlimited credit. It is one thing to oblige a few regular custom-ers, whom the trader is sure will pay up at the end of the month. It is another thing to grant 'pay later' terms to every customer asking for them.

A trader must buy the goods he puts into stock, and pay for them long before most of them will be sold. Much of his capital will be tied up in goods even if he confines his busi-ness to cash trading only. When in addition the customers want to settle next month, and there is no money coming in to pay the bills, the problem is acute. It is not only the lack of money to finance and keep the business ticking over. Many small firms know only too well from bitter experience that not all customers honour their credit commitments. Bad debts, un-paid bills which are unlikely ever to be cleared, eat into profits.

A large firm can insist on credit references. Before a single pound's worth of goods exchange hands, these references are checked. Checking and verifying takes time and time costs money. Small shops tended to avoid trouble, only to court disaster when the account holder disappears without paying.

The Credit Card

Promising one man businesses sensed that credit was the key to expansion, yet they were reluctant to offer it, with so many pitfalls. The credit card changed all this.

A credit card is a piece of plastic with personal details, name and number, imprinted on it, bearing the holder's signature, issued by a credit card agency or organisation. When the holder calls in to buy and to use his card the information is trans-ferred to an invoice prepared by the shopkeeper on the spot. These invoices are despatched to the credit card headquarters by the shopkeeper who is either paid immediately, or at the end of the month. The bills in turn are resorted and posted to the cardholder once each month, with a covering account de-tailing each transaction, and the total amount due.

This is the outline of a plan which has been operated in the United States for many years. It is a sound and good system which gives cash to the shopkeeper and credit to the customer. It has to be paid for. Originally a cardholder paid a sizeable fee, normally a few pounds, for the privilege of belonging to the scheme. The trader was charged a commission on all sales completed through the card system. These two sources of income were sufficient, once the credit card was established, to meet all expenses, pay off any bad debts or fraudulent use, and still leave a profit.

There is a limit to the number of potential customers, pre-pared to buy a card for an annual subscription. Cards appeal mainly to travellers, and to company employees with expense accounts.

Something was needed to crack this tight circle of credit card users. The breakthrough came from the Barclay Bank organisation when they introduced the Barclaycard. Aimed at outrivalling its rivals, it emphasised two points. Anybody could hold a Barclaycard, and the card was free. The trader still paid his fees, but the customer paid nothing. This was the master stroke needed to introduce credit cards to a whole new sector of the population. Now the market became wide open since anyone could hold a card at no cost to themselves. Ideal for emergencies, it spread quickly to clothes shops, restaurants and petrol stations, and the whole range of supporting shops and services.

The advantages of the credit card thundered from advertisements; you could shop at tens of thousands of shops without money. All the month's purchase could be settled with one monthly cheque, at no extra charge. Not only was the card free, but also it produced cash with or without a chequebook at the Bank's branches.

Why should a trader give up a portion of his profits in order to accommodate credit customers? This has to be answered in terms of commercial economics. If the Latest Gown Ltd or the Green Parrot Restaurant can increase their trade, and aim at an hitherto untapped public, then a percentage of sales is a small price to pay. Certain larger multiple organisations swung to its support, when they costed the service against providing a full credit scheme of their own. Cards are cheaper and there are no bad debts.

A well advertised card system creates its own side benefits. Card holders search out firms that display the credit card sign and they tend to spend more and choose better quality goods compared with the cash customer. All they need is a little rectangle of plastic; there is little fear of them leaving purchases behind while they go home for chequebook or cash.

These are points stressed by the credit card firms. Naturally they ignore the disadvantages. First there are competing credit cards so that the shop attempting to stay abreast needs to display six or more signs. Credit cards can make shopping too easy. Cards cannot help the man or woman without money sense. Easy to use, simple to spend with, they could produce sky-high bills in no time. This too is recognised by the card firms, who turn it to their advantage. Instead of paying off the total sum due, as little as ten per cent down will keep the account open, with a service fee calculated on the outstanding balance. This additional charge is as expensive, but no more so, than other instalment credit loans.

Complete freedom of choice is the one thing the card holder lacks. Large stores with their own credit facilities will have nothing to do with them. Of course you can open an account at every such store, so losing the advantages of a single card and bill. Limited outlets which accept cards could mean that money must still be carried. It takes time to persuade enough stores of the advantages of credit living.

This is one of the main problems facing the established firms; at least it prevents more competitors entering the field. Until there are enough card holders, the share of business for each participating store is small. It may not seem worth the trouble of joining in. Until there are enough firms accepting cards, new card holders are likely to defer joining. This vicious circle was broken by Barclaycard, when they made cards free. At least the cardholder cannot lose, even if he never uses it.

Prices on credit tend to be more expensive than cash. Petrol is a typical competitive commodity; premiums in the form of cash reductions or trading stamps are commonplace. These apply only to cash buyers—no garage can afford to pay the percentage on credit sales too. It is less obvious in the typical British shop where there is no tradition of haggling. The average shopper pays full price. It is worth checking that he pays no more when he uses his card.

Credit cards are here to stay. Credit chains are international. Money in many countries with one piece of plastic, and ' round the world ' credit is with us now.

Credit for the consumer is matched by a similar story for the shopkeeper, distributor or manufacturer. They all depend on credit finance, partly provided by the wholesaler, and more often by a finance house. New plant and machinery stimulate trade. They are probably financed on credit.

Hiring

Credit with a difference is one way of looking at hiring. Firms have grown rich in providing for hire tents or dress suits, cars and drinking glasses. It has become common to sign a contract for a year or more to hire a television set. At first sight these hiring fees, paid weekly or monthly seem not unlike payments on hire purchase or extended credit. One difference is that instalments never come to an end. Month after month, the charges continue until the goods are returned. Charges may fall after the first few years; they never disappear. Many of the goods offered under these hiring plans have a low value second-hand.

Part of the hiring contract promises that instant repair or replacement is guaranteed, should this become necessary. Convenience for the man intent on never missing a television episode becomes an essential to the commercial traveller with a hire car. Most of the successful firms, for television or cars, are nationwide or at least cover a region densely. While one particular car or television set will be unlikely to fail more than three times a year, the total number of hirings ensures full employment to maintenance staff. Hiring permits instant replacement of new for old, by cancelling one contract and signing another. More expensive than straightforward purchase or credit, it can be cheaper when repairs are taken into account.

Advertisements can be seen in papers offering large sums of money on loan. They stem from two sources—finance houses and moneylenders. Finance companies are willing to lend to professional men and women with steady salaries, and an ability to pay back promptly. They charge about the same as a bank 'personal loan'. Most of the larger finance companies are in any case now owned by the banks.

Finance houses are moneylenders pure and simple, following the same trade, as the '£5 to £500 without security' brigade, the moneylenders of popular image. It is nonsense that a moneylender will part with his money without any security. If you live in rented rooms, has a casual job, and have been there only a month, your chance of borrowing £5 is practically nil. If you are a householder, with a steady job, then you will probably stand a good chance of borrowing as much as you can afford to repay. No security, except for a good job and a steady record is really very good security. Moneylenders charge a lot for their money. By law, only more than 48 per cent each year is considered excessive.

Moneylenders will find money in a hurry, if you are an established citizen with a good job. Pawnbrokers can help if you have valuable goods. Their interest rates are very very high. The advice 'steer clear' is the best you could be given.

THINGS TO DO

1 Examine a hire purchase contract. Calculate the true rate of interest. What are the conditions which restrict the sale of the goods?
2 Compare the true annual interest rates for borrowing £100 through some of the methods outlined. Include the electricity or gas boards' credit schemes, at least one department store, and a moneylender.
3 Discuss the statement 'The only people who can borrow money are those who already have it'. How true is this in ordinary cases?

4 Ask your bank manager how much he would be willing to lend and for how long, if you wanted to buy (a) a new car; (b) central heating for your home.

5 List the advantages and disadvantages of buying on credit.

6 Discuss with a credit card trader the advantages and disadvantages of his membership in the scheme. Ask especially why he particularly found membership an advantage, why he joined in the first instance, and if experience has changed his views.

7 You decide to obtain a credit card. What details must you give the firm, before they will consider you? Once issued, what are the problems you will face, when you use the card, and how will you overcome them?

8 Discuss the trend towards living on credit. Is it necessary, and is it desirable?

9 Is it true that we are moving towards a cashless society?

10 Complete a survey of your local shopping centres. Distinguish between the credit schemes the shops offer.

Chapter Six **Life Assurance**

The Idea and Early Days of Life Assurance

Man protects himself against dangerous and unpleasant things. He wears thick clothes in winter as defence against the cold, he arranges that his home is weatherproof, and a cut finger is quickly bandaged as a protection against dirt. Protection is natural, and extends to the whole family. Man tries to preserve the family unit, and so establishes security.

In most families the husband is the wage-earner, providing food and shelter with his earnings. This is the story of the human race from the dawn of civilisation when the hunter went out to forage for his wife and children. Should the wage-earner die, the family would be left unprotected. Wise men insure themselves against this possibility. Life assurance rather than insurance, because payment by the company is bound to occur, sooner or later. Assurance policies are payable when either the holder dies, or he reaches a certain age. One or the other event must take place, so assurance is unlike an insurance policy which only pays when there is a loss or accident that may, or may not, happen.

Life assurance exists to pay claims. It is a contract which undertakes to pay, and contains three main essentials. The ' proposal ' which is a form on which the particulars of the person to be assured are given, including age and health records. The 'policy', or contract which is the legal agreement between the assured and the assurance company which is drawn up on the basis of the information in the proposal. The ' premium ' which is the instalment payable each year, for a fixed number of years assuring a cash sum in return.

Life assurance at the beginning of the eighteenth century was a gamble. The idea of setting aside some money or making

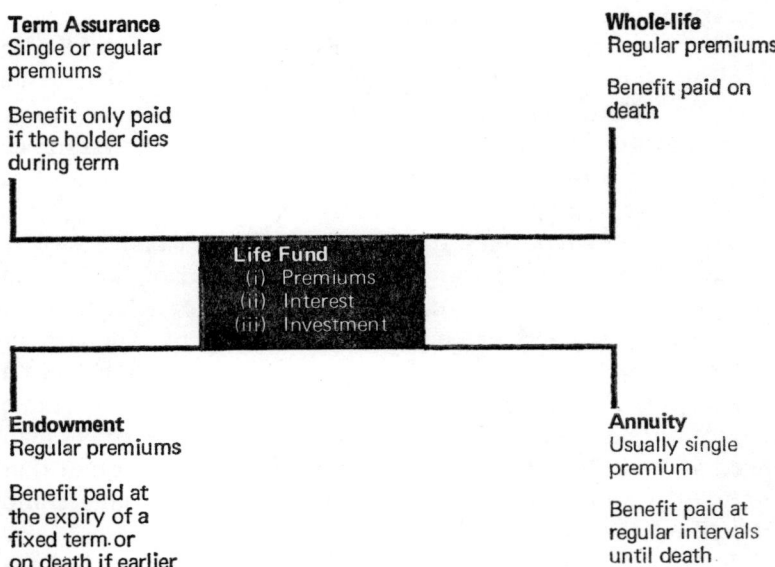

Term Assurance
Single or regular
premiums

Benefit only paid
if the holder dies
during term

Whole-life
Regular premiums

Benefit paid on
death

Life Fund
(i) Premiums
(ii) Interest
(iii) Investment

Endowment
Regular premiums

Benefit paid at
the expiry of a
fixed term or
on death if earlier

Annuity
Usually single
premium

Benefit paid at
regular intervals
until death

provision for dependents is not new. The Romans kept back a share of their soldiers' pay, which was paid out after the battle on retirement in order that he could start up in some trade on his own. Should he be killed, his family received the money, and so were not destitute.

Perhaps the first life insurance policies which bear some resemblance to the contracts of today were issued by companies to protect ships' crews. In those days the chances of being captured by pirates were quite high and there was always the ransom to be paid. Insurance provided the bounty demanded, and the poor unfortunates without cover were more often than not made to walk the plank. It was not worthwhile keeping them alive, if the money was hard to obtain. Later insurance policies were extended to cover death from any cause while at sea.

In the sixteenth century policies were commonplace for short terms from a few months to several years. They were taken out to provide security against the payment of a loan, or maybe in those days of difficult communication, in case accidents occurred on a long journey.

Life assurance as it is known today began in the eighteenth century. James Dodson, a teacher of mathematics at Christ's Hospital, London, tried to insure his life with a company known as the ' Amicable Society for a Perpetual Life Assurance Office '. Unfortunately it only accepted business from persons aged 9 to 45, and James Dodson was 46.

The idea in Dodson's day was little better than a sweepstake. When you died your family had no idea of how much they might collect. It all depended on business—the number who had died that year and the size of the pool. The cost of entering this lottery was a haphazard affair. Premiums were a sheer guess, and no matter what your age, you paid the same amount. This was obviously unfair, and the man or woman aged 45 had the better of the bargain. Those older found that premiums were so prohibitively high, that they virtually could not afford life assurance.

James Dodson did more than anyone previously to put life assurance on some scientific basis. He worked out, more by luck than judgement, a table which calculated the average number of years ' expectation of life ' at any age. He then calculated the amount that would have to be paid into the common fund, to meet payments on death, or on the reaching of a given age; every policyholder was bound to do one or the other. The common fund could meet claims from the beginning. It was a mutual or cooperative venture, each member of the society sharing the risks, and the profits.

The new aspect of this pool was the ' level ' premium. The likelihood of payment from the fund is much lower when the assured is young, and becomes more and more probable as he grows older. A fair system would be to charge quite a small premium in youth, and to increase it gradually as the members of the society aged. There is always the possibility that such premiums could grow so large that the members could not afford to pay them. A ' level ' premium is a fixed rate each year, for the whole period of the assurance. In the earlier years, the participants pay considerably more than would be expected from them. As the policy progresses, they pay less than is necessary, and over the whole period of the assurance the over-payments and underpayments balance out.

The powers-that-be were convinced that the scheme could not work. In fact quite the opposite was the case; it became so successful that it was forced to pay out a large money surplus as a bonus.

All good ideas catch on, and the unprincipled soon moved in for an easy killing. Most of the money paid into such funds stays there for many years until the policies mature. Only an occasional claim will disturb the mounting balance of money. This is ideal for the dishonest and fraudulent, who in the early nineteenth century took full advantage of the situation. The government stepped in and framed regulations which guarantee that all assurance companies today are bound by laws which safeguard the investor.

Life assurance policies will eventually be paid. To meet the claims, a life assurance firm or life office, must have sufficient reserves, known as the life fund. This common pool of money is filled from a number of sources. Obviously the premiums, as they come in each year are one such source, and the main one. Most of the money as it is paid in will not be needed for many years. It is carefully invested in different fields where the capital sum is not at risk. These investments gather interest which swells the life fund. Careful management of these invest-ments can also produce an increase in the capital, so that when they are sold they fetch more than was paid in the first place. Property is one example of investment. The rents provide interest each year, and when the property is sold the value will almost always be more than its cost years earlier.

Management of the life fund is a matter of skill and judge-ment. There must always be enough money in the kitty to pay out claims, without selling any of the investments. Forced sel-ling of stocks and shares can well produce a loss. On the other hand, most of the fund should be invested. Money lying idle is interest wasted. Good management will produce a surplus of funds, over and above that needed to pay off all possible claims. How this surplus is used depends upon the type of life assurance company. Mutual companies divide all their surplus between existing policyholders; proprietary offices divide the amount between policyholders and shareholders, although the lion's share is added to the policies.

Types of Policy

There are four main types of policies. The cheapest of them all is term assurance, which should really be called term insurance, for these policies do not always result in a claim.

A term assurance contract is for a fixed number of years. If the holder dies within this period then benefit becomes payable. It is possible to buy this type of policy either by paying a lump sum, once and for all, or by agreeing to subscribe equal instalments each year.

Term assurance provides protection very cheaply when it is most needed. It would for instance help a family, with young children and a large mortgage if the husband died. Benefits can be paid in a number of ways: (a) as a fixed lump sum no matter when during the period of the policy the holder should die; (b) as a reducing lump sum—in a twenty year policy for instance £1000 might be paid for each year still left to run; (c) as an annual payment of say £1000 for the remaining term of the policy; (d) as a combination of the annual payments and a lump sum.

It is usual to arrange one of these policies with a single payment and reducing benefits, linked to a mortgage. Should the holder die, the policy pays the amount outstanding, and the family at least has a home with no further payments due.

Term assurance then is really designed to provide benefits when they can help most, such as the crucial period when a family still has young children at school. Fortunately most term assurance policies expire unused.

Next and slightly more expensive is whole-life assurance. These policies are payable on the death of the holder; only when he dies will any benefit be due, and no earlier no matter how long he may live. They may be arranged to allow premiums to cease at retirement age, or to be carried on for life. All whole-life policies eventually result in claims, although the majority will be delayed for many years. This gap between taking out the policy, and its payment means that the annual premium can be very low.

Endowment assurance is a savings policy. It is a combination between life insurance, with payment of an agreed lump sum should the holder die while the policy is in force, and a savings bank which promises to pay the full amount at the end of a given number of years. It differs from a whole life policy in that as long as the policyholder survives he will receive a lump sum at the end of the term. Part of each premium is put on one side for possible early repayment; the bulk of each instalment forms a saving fund which is paid out on maturity of the policy.

Fourthly there is the annuity. This is an income for life, which may be bought either by a single payment or by instalments over some years. An annuity is a kind of pension. On death, the policy lapses. When an assurance policy matures, there is often the option of either taking the value in cash or investing the proceeds in an annuity. Annuities can be arranged on two or more lives; husband and wife is a common combination. There is always the possibility that an annuity will only be called upon for one or two payments before the holder dies. It can be arranged so that there are a minimum number of annual payments, and it is possible for each yearly payment to increase as a hedge against the rise in the cost of living.

Choosing a Policy

Life assurance is a matter of choice, to provide the best possible protection for the family within the limits of one's wages. More protection is needed when the family is young, and it is at this time that wages are low. As the family grows up, less protection is needed, although now the average family will be in a position to buy more assurance.

There are many assurance companies, each in competition with the others, and the benefits they pay vary widely. The cost, for say £1000 in 20 years time, for a young man aged 25 can vary by pounds each year.

Partly this variation is due to the management expertise of the life fund. It also depends upon the scale of commission that they pay to their representatives (some do not pay any commission at all). Advertising, and the range of risks that they are prepared to accept all affect the profits, and so in turn the amount that they are able to afford to pay.

One solution is to go to an assurance broker, who will advise and suggest four or five suitable companies. Another plan is to answer advertisements by a number of companies, and to write for quotations. While one company is the cheapest for certain kinds of policy, another firm may be most competitive for the type that you have in mind.

Assurance through One's Life

Every family should be covered by life assurance. As families grow in size and grow older, their needs change. It is a good idea to look at the protection they have bought every five years or so, although it never pays to cancel life assurance. Should changes become necessary then it is best to keep the policies already in force, and add to them as required.

A young man or woman without a family could probably afford to take out a large amount of assurance. The cost of a policy is cheapest when one is young—the only doubt is if the cost each year will be too much, as one grows older and takes on more commitments.

Let us look at the Brown family from soon after marriage, until the husband dies fifty years later. Each period of their life will show the purpose of a particular type of policy.

Mr and Mrs Brown married when they were 22 years old and bought a house on mortgage, owing the building society £5000. They could not afford the regular life policies then, but they were just able to manage term assurance, with its very low premiums. They looked carefully at their position, wanting as much benefit as possible for the smallest outlay. It was important they thought that should Mr Brown die, then the mortgage ought to be paid, and Mrs Brown should receive an annual income.

They bought a mortgage protection policy which took care

of all their money worries on the house. They also invested in a term assurance policy, paying yearly instalments over 25 years. Should Mr Brown die, his wife would benefit by receiving £5000.

Six years later when the Browns were 28 years old, they looked at their assurance again. Now they had two children 4 years and 1 year old, and in the meantime Mr Brown had been promoted. They could afford to spend more each year so they purchased a second term assurance policy. Still very cheap, this one would pay at the rate of £100 each year for every year from the time Mr Brown died until Mrs Brown was 58 years old. By then the children would be grown up. There was a little money left over, so they decided to buy a whole-life policy which would have a benefit value of £10,000. This, the cheapest of real assurance policies, might cause them to go on paying instalments for 40 or 50 years. Far from being a millstone round their necks, it was a piece of paper that any bank manager would recognise as a valuable security, and accept should they ever need a loan.

Mr Brown revised his insurances again on his 33rd birthday. There were now three children, aged 4, 6 and 9 and they were well provided for by two term assurances and a whole life policy. This then was a reasonable time to begin saving. Mr Brown chose a 25 year endowment assurance in the sum of £2000. An expensive policy to choose but if he lived he would be collecting the benefit when he was 58 years old, still young enough to enjoy it. By then, his family would have left home.

Both Mr and Mrs Brown took out further endowment assurances at the age of 40, for a 25 year term. These would be due for payment when Mr Brown retired.

Mr and Mrs Brown led a healthy, happy life. They passed the 58 year milestone, and their term assurance expired unused. They did not mind that the money paid in premiums had shown no practical result. The protection and the comfort that money could bring in difficult times had been there.

Mr Brown cashed in his endowment policy at 58, and since he was still at work in a good job, he did not particularly need the money. The whole amount was invested in an annuity, jointly for himself and his wife, to begin at the age of 65. It was also arranged that there would be a minimum of five annual payments, and that each year's pension was to be a little larger than the year before.

Mr Brown retired at 65 and he and his wife cashed their endowment assurances which had matured. Mrs Brown took hers in cash, and they both went off on a six month's round-the-world cruise. Mr Brown changed his cash sum into another joint annuity. With these two annuities, his state and works pension, and the retirement capital sum from his firm, he was well provided for.

Mr Brown died when he was 72 years old. The whole-life policy whose first instalment had been paid over 44 years before, was now cashed, and came to Mrs Brown. £10,000 invested made up in money terms for the loss of Mr Brown's pension which died with him. Mrs Brown still continued to benefit from both annuities.

Profits

Schemes such as this provide protection whatever should happen when it is needed. The company representative is able to give detailed advice; what is right for one family may not suit another. Life assurance is long term financial planning and needs careful professional advice.

There are two types of life policies—'with profits' and 'without profits'. A good insurance company will take care of its investments, and should show a handsome increase on the size of its investments in the life fund. These profits are shared out, much of it going towards the policies that are labelled 'with profits'. Policies without profits pay only the sum insured, and they are passed by when bonuses are announced. On the other hand 'without profit' policies are far cheaper. They may be economical at the time, but they suffer when costs are rising. £1000 will be worth far less than it sounds in twenty, thirty or forty years time.

All companies offer 'with profit' policies which are more expensive because the final benefit is greater, but they are

Mr and Mrs Brown's assurance

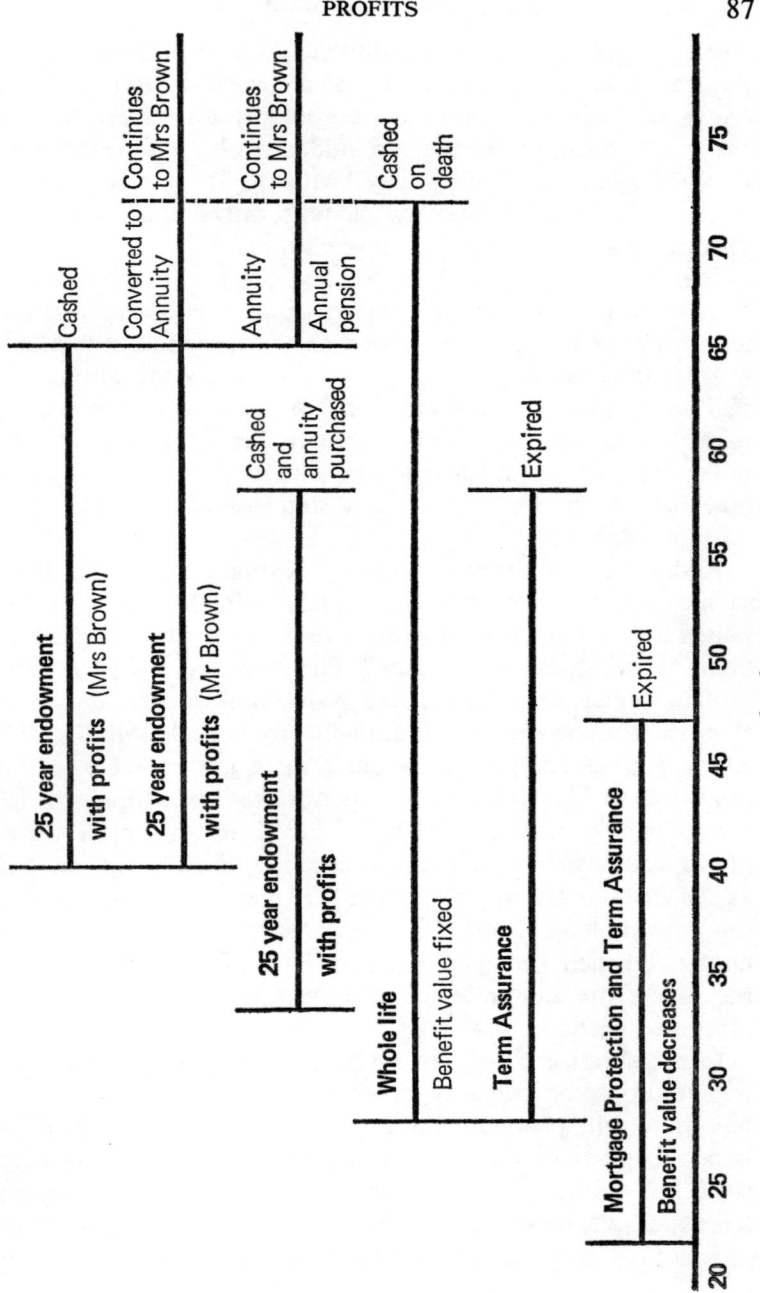

better for all long term insurances. Less insurance cover is purchased for a given premium so if the policy holder should die in the first few years, his next of kin will receive less. In the longer term, as bonuses are added to the policy, there will be more in return. This is why ' with profit ' policies are best reserved for middle age; the savings rather than immediate protection is then uppermost in one's mind.

It is easier to persuade people that life assurance is needed than to convince them that saving through endowment assurance makes sense. Looking ahead they can see that it would be a good idea to add to their pension but they are not so sure that endowments are a good buy. No one can be positive that they will always be healthy. Once a life insurance contract policy has been sold, the company cannot cancel it. No matter how sick one becomes, the policy stands which is itself an important safeguard.

Endowment assurance requires regular premiums. Good savings habits begin early which may help the less well-disciplined individuals. But why not save through a building society or invest in stocks and shares? The sum assured on a ' with profits ' policy is roughly equal to the total in premiums paid. Bonuses after twenty five years will probably double this. The endowment is competitive because there are valuable income tax benefits. This is the edge which makes the actual cost less than it would seem. There is an added advantage. A whole-life or endowment policy will eventually be paid out. As long as the instalments are maintained, it remains perfect security for a bank loan. Most life companies can arrange loans to holders on their own policies, and this will be true even when the banks are not able to help their customers because of official restrictions.

Life assurance is inflexible. Once committed to a policy the best results come at maturity. They may be surrendered earlier but there will probably be a loss. Later in life such a loss is not so great, but it will never do so well as keeping it for the full term. There is an alternative if premiums have become too expensive, but the money is not needed at once. Conversion into a fully paid up policy can be arranged. All the money already paid in continues to earn bonuses at a reduced rate and a smaller life cover is maintained until the maturity date.

It is quite impossible to forecast the value of a 'with profits' policy twenty to thirty years ahead. The only information available is a table of the past records of different companies showing how they fared in the past. As each new table is prepared, relative positions of the top ten change. Only consistency can help there.

Life assurance business has been growing at a spectacular pace as year after year, ordinary people have been putting more and more of their savings individually into life assurance. They have also been entrusting their future security to the life assurance business on a group basis. Life offices administer many of the group pension schemes, which provide retirement benefits to all the employees in a particular firm. Four million people are members of such schemes.

The total assured under life policies of all kinds is more than £30,000 millions. Annuities account for £1250 millions a year. The life funds of all the companies total 10,000 million pounds. Many millions more will be needed to pay all the claims and annuities as the years go by. Where will these missing millions come from? Partly from future premiums under contracts now in force, but only partly. Much of the missing money must come from income on investments.

About 60 per cent of all life assurance investments are in the fixed income areas—loans to property owners, the government and companies. They produce good returns but they are not proof against inflation. Only the remaining 40 per cent is in stocks and shares, lands and buildings, and other investments which move upwards reflecting the cost of living. To overcome some of the dangers of being left behind, there have been moves which link life assurance directly with investment in stocks and shares. Most of the premiums are put into areas where it is hoped that the value of the investment rather than the income from it will appreciate. It is early yet to see if these moves will succeed. Short term investment values move up or down; only gradually does long term appreciation make itself felt.

Building societies too are linking with assurance companies to take advantage of the income tax bonus. It is now possible to benefit from the security and high interest of a building society account, and collect free life assurance cover at the same time.

Life assurance is unique. It takes on the 'uncertain certainty'—death, and sees that those prudent enough to plan forward for the future, are sheltered financially.

THINGS TO DO

1 Plan a life assurance policy scheme that would suit you now, and in five years time. Plan a similar scheme for your parents. Obtain quotations for more than one company to see how much it would cost you.

2 What is your opinion of life assurance as a way to save?

3 This section has dwelt entirely with 'ordinary' policies. There are also 'home service' (industrial section) policies, which are maintained by the representative calling at your home for the premiums every week or month. In general the benefits are lower than ordinary policies. What are the advantages of such policies?

4 What are the changes in life assurance needed when (a) a new baby arrives; (b) children leave school; (c) you get promotion at work; (d) your mortgage has been paid off?

5 Life assurance helps the economy. Consider how life assurance funds help commerce and government.

6 Compare 'with profit' and 'without profit' policies for ages from 25 to 30 years, if the capital sum is £1000, and the period is 25 years. How much cheaper are whole-life policies?

7 Everyone needs life assurance. Discuss this, and explain why so many families who could afford it have not bothered with life assurance protection.

Chapter Seven Stocks and Shares

The Stock Exchange

How does the Stock Exchange appear to you? Remote, something in the city, where men with money make and lose fortunes? In fact, the Stock Exchange affects every one of us. It is an essential part of the life of the country in business, industry and Government itself. It touches the welfare of you and me.

Investment is vital to the country's prosperity. Money is required for services in the community, such as schools and hospitals, and to expand industry so creating more jobs. Money is needed to smooth the flow of goods and services both at home and to the export markets abroad. Large amounts of money, known as capital, are needed by governments and industry in order to help finance their expenditure on such a scale. The Stock Exchange provides the ways and means for raising money, issuing in return stocks and shares. It provides a market place where the buyers and sellers of such shares can carry on their business through their stockbrokers.

Stockbrokers operate within the Exchange under strict rules designed for the protection of investors in stocks and shares. No official body fixes the prices; they are determined solely by the laws of supply and demand in a free and active market.

Nearly ten thousand securities (the name given to the many types of investments with which the Stock Exchange is concerned) are officially quoted. Their total value is more than 130,000 million pounds. Of this total the British Government is responsible for 18,000 million pounds. Each month 500,000 transactions take place involving 2600 million pounds. A lot of money all based on trust.

It was in the seventeenth century that the Government and a

number of trading enterprises began to raise money. In those days the public were invited to subscribe for a share in the stock or venture. Stocks and shares were issued and as they were bought and sold on an increasing scale, a market developed with brokers whose object was to bring buyers and sellers together. They used to meet near the Royal Exchange in the City of London, and then they moved into local coffee houses. To this day their uniformed attendants are known as waiters.

In 1771 a meeting of these stockbrokers decided that they needed a home of their own. From this simple start has grown, as Britain's trade and commerce has grown, the great financial market that exists today.

It is possible to visit the Stock Exchange, and from the Visitors' Gallery one can look down at this amazing market place. There will be seen the members of the Stock Exchange hurrying to and fro. There are two types of member: brokers and jobbers. Stockbrokers are the people that you approach should you wish to buy or sell shares. They earn their living from the commission which they charge on all orders. Jobbers are the wholesalers of the Stock Exchange. They do not deal directly with the public but only with a stockbroker member.

There are over 3400 members of the Stock Exchange. Of these, about 520 are jobbers, divided among 30 firms. No jobber could hope to know all about 10,000 securities. Instead they specialise in a certain category, and study them carefully. There will be more than one firm dealing in a particular group, in competition with other jobbers, and making the best prices they can to attract stockbrokers to buy and sell with them.

The Types of Securities

Why is there a need for stocks and shares, and for that matter what is the difference? These securities are divisible into two basic groups.

Gilt-edged stocks, debentures and loan capital are issued at a fixed rate of interest, and the borrowers often, although not always agree to repay on a certain date the face value of the stock or even a little more. These securities pay their interest at regular intervals, usually every six months, and it is relatively safe. The capital or money invested will normally be repaid on a given date in the future. Some stocks, although they guarantee a regular income through interest, are not repayable at a fixed date. They may possibly be bought back by the issuing agency after a given time, but there is no certainty that this will be so. When you wish to recover your money, such stocks will have to be sold through the Stock Exchange; you may get back more or less than you paid in the first place.

Loans to the Government, nationalised industries, local authorities and the like are very safe indeed. Interest rates are a little lower than on the debentures and loan capital of the larger industrial firms. These securities are normally secured, or in a manner of speaking mortgaged, on the plant and machinery of the firm. If they fail to pay the interest on time, or delay repaying the loan, debenture holders have the right to force the sale of this land and machinery, to pay for all the interest outstanding, and the repayment of the loan.

All these are fixed interest investments, just like National Savings, building society accounts and other bank saving schemes. Interest rates are higher, because these securities are more difficult to buy and sell. In their regular payments they are almost perfectly safe. Invariably the capital is repaid on time. Inflation however does mean that £100 now could be worth less than half that figure in twenty years time. This is important. Income stays steady, but the real worth of capital decreases with inflation.

The second basic group is made up of preference and ordinary shares. With stocks and debentures you were lending your money to the business; in this group you are buying a share in the firm. You, and the other shareholders are the owners of the company.

Dividends are paid at a fixed rate of interest to preference shareholders, after all expenses and interest on loan stock and debentures have been paid. The dividend ranks after loan stock, so a higher interest rate will usually be received.

Ordinary shareholders share in the profit remaining after all other expenses and dividends have been paid. It would be impractical for thousands of shareholders to each have an active part in the business, so every year they meet together at the Annual General Meeting. Here they elect directors, and it is the board of directors which make the day-to-day and long term policy decisions within the company. The board also recommends the dividend which is to be paid on the ordinary shares. Shareholders have one vote for each share. In this respect it is unlike an election of a Member of Parliament, where each elector has only one vote. The more shares held in a company, the larger the number of votes.

The profits of a company almost always vary from year to year. Profits are the source of money paid out as dividends, so that in good years the dividend could rise. Conversely in poor years the amount paid out will drop, or the directors may recommend that there should be no dividend at all. Not all the profits are paid out. Some will be transferred to reserve, either for a specific new project or simply as a safeguard should things go badly.

More investors will want shares if the profit record and the dividends rise steadily each year. Erratic performances, and firms which turn in lower profits figures will not be in such keen demand.

The Price of Shares
It is this buying and selling, and the changing fashions of the public and shareholders, which affects the price of shares. If there are more offered than can be found buyers, then the price will drop, while if there are less for sale than are wanted, the price will rise.

There are only a fixed number of shares issued in a company. They cannot be made or cancelled on the spot, and of this number, there may be say 5000 shares available on any one day. Perhaps a financial journalist selects one company for special comment. The number of would-be buyers quickly grows. The price rises. in the hope that supply and demand balance. This can happen in two ways. First, because the price is rising, some of the would-be buyers have second thoughts and decide that they no longer want these shares. Second, the

higher price may tempt some existing shareholders into the
market, offering for sale shares that they originally had no
intention of parting with. Eventually the number of buyers
and sellers balances, and the price stops its movement.

A similar situation occurs in reverse when the price drops.
It stops some sellers from disposing of their shares, and causes
buyers to come into the market because the price being asked
for the shares looks cheap.

Once the shares have been placed on sale by the company
there is no obligation for them to buy them back. Indeed they
were sold in the first place to provide money which in turn
was put into land, buildings and plant. There is no money to
take back these shares yet no one wishes to tie up their capital
for ever. These shares will sooner or later be sold. Instead of
putting an advertisement in the newspaper, hoping to find someone willing to buy them, with all the haggling over price, and
the trouble to transfer them, they can be sold through the
Stock Exchange. A market place, a free and active market,
designed to take all the difficulties out of transfer at an
economical rate.

Buying Shares

Let us take a fictional company, and imagine that you wish
to buy some shares. Only the company is invented—the stages
are real enough.

You write or telephone your stockbroker and ask him to buy
for you 100 ordinary shares in High Street Stores Limited.
Your broker, or a member of his firm, will enter the floor of
the Stock Exchange, and call on a number of jobbers who
deal in this share. From one he will be offered a price of 310
to 315, and from another a price of 313 to 316. These figures
are quoted in pence, and two prices are mentioned because at
this stage the jobber does not know if the broker wishes to buy
or to sell. Your stockbroker does not necessarily go back to
the first jobber, but may call on a third firm. Here he is quoted
311 to 315, decides to complete the deal, and says ' I buy 100 '.
A note is made by the jobber in his notebook, another note in
the broker's book, and that is all. No documents are ex-

Buying shares

Telephone stockbroker
|
Broker calls on jobbers
|
Price agreed
|
Contract note
|
Payment made
|
Share certificate

Share ownership

Share ━━━━━ Receive dividends
ownership

━━━━━ Attend
annual general meeting

━━━━━ Allotment
extra shares 'free'

━━━━━ Capitalisation
extra shares bought
as of right.

changed. Not even a handshake, for their motto is 'My word is my bond'.

When the jobber quotes a price, he is bound to accept any reasonable size order at that level. Since he has no way of knowing in advance which way the order will be placed or for how many shares, he must be an astute businessman. Even if he does not particularly want to make a market in a certain share, he must maintain his competitive position. He hopes that the difference in prices will be enough to enable him to earn a living, and if prices never changed this 'jobbers turn' would be handsome reward. We have seen that share prices go up or down. In addition our jobber who has just sold 100 shares at 315 may not have any in stock. He will then have to go out and buy them. This he hopes to do by the Account Day, which comes round every two or three weeks. On these days all transactions must be completed. If he can buy those 100 shares at 314 or less he has made a profit; if they cost more than 315 he will make a loss. Whatever the position and price, he will buy the shares to make good his bargain.

On the day you buy the shares the broker will send you a contract note. This is a legal document of purchase which sets out the following details.

The number of shares and the name of the company, and if you have bought or sold. The price, which in this case is 315 and the consideration or total price £315. Now the expenses of a buying transaction are listed. The transfer stamp which is a Government duty, totalling £3.50. The actual rate is one per cent rounded up. Shareholders names, addresses and holdings are listed by the Company Registrar, on the Register of Shareholdings. At one time there was a transfer fee, for adding details to the register. Most companies have abolished this charge, and our firm of High Street Stores Limited is one of them. There is a charge for a 10p contract stamp. Finally there is the Stockbroker's commission for buying your shares. This is at a fixed rate of $1\frac{1}{4}$ per cent, but there is a minimum of £4 for deals of modest size, which is charged in this case. The shares which cost £315 have incurred costs of £3.50, 10p and £4, making the total £322.60. One other item appears on the contract note. This is the date of settlement. Your cheque must be in the broker's hands, and cleared, by then.

In time your broker forwards a share certificate, your evidence of ownership. Some time will elapse before the certificate arrives, although you are the legal owner from the day the shares were bought, and you can sell them at any time you wish.

High Street Stores Limited Ordinary Shares are of nominal value £1. This denomination is of academic interest. It becomes important only when the company declares a dividend. In the first year you own the shares they declare a final dividend of 10 per cent. This means that 10 per cent of the nominal value is to be paid out, or 10p on each share. The company has no way of knowing how much you actually paid for each share, and indeed is little interested. They know that you are now part-owner with 100 shares, and there are probably 1000 other shareholders, who will have bought at different prices and times.

The company will pay your dividend after deduction of income tax by warrant, which is no more than a cheque. Attached to the warrant is a tax deduction voucher, which may be used to reclaim tax, if you do not have to pay it.

Each year the Company will send their Annual Report, complete with balance sheet, profit and loss account, and a notice summoning you to the Annual General Meeting. When times are good, these meetings are poorly attended unless the

D

directors lay on some entertainment for their shareholders. After a bad year the meeting can be stormy, and the directors may not be re-elected.

High Street Stores Limited paid an interim dividend in the second year of 5 per cent. This is done when the directors wish to pay something to their shareholders without waiting for the end of the financial year. It was followed by a final dividend of 9 per cent, so cheques totalling £15 less income tax were received. Your yield, or the percentage that you receive based on the cost price of the shares was a little over 4 per cent that year. Far less than a building society, but you believe that the dividend will be even more next year, and already the market price has risen.

Three years have passed, and one day a large envelope arrives with two documents. Subject to a general meeting of shareholders, they propose to allot or give you one free bonus share for every share that you already hold, and in addition they offer you the right to buy one further share at £1 for every ten original shares you hold. You can buy ten shares in all for a total of £10, and you will also receive 100 shares by way of right.

Why should the company go to all this trouble? Shares are ' split ', or bonus shares are given free of charge, when the company feels that the share price is too high. No extra money has been put into the business, so one free share for each one held should mean that the share price is halved. Many Stock Exchange investors believe that high share price makes a share dear, and a low price cheap. Nothing could be further from the truth.

Shares issued for cash to existing shareholders are an easy way for a company to get more money. The price at which these new shares are offered is usually a bargain, and the rights issue is successful.

At the moment that the news was released, the shares stood at 410 so that their total value was £410. After the announcement, you own 210 shares which should be worth £420 altogether, including the £10 you have paid. This would mean a price of 200. Next day the shares were being traded at 210.

This difference of 10p, worth £21 on the 210 shares, is explained by the extra activity as buyers came looking for shares. The rights and bonus issue brought High Street Stores Limited into the limelight.

One day these shares will be sold. Much the same procedure will be followed as when they were bought. There is no government duty, but stockbroker and contract note fees must be paid. In addition, if shares show a gain in value, the difference between the total paid and the total received may be subject to capital gains tax.

Choosing a Share

More than two and a half million people invest directly through the Stock Exchange. Everyone who owns an insurance policy, contributes to a trade union or pension scheme, or who has a savings deposit in a bank is an indirect investor. These organisations invest much of their money in stocks and shares.

As an individual investor your own particular circumstances must be considered. Do you want a high income with little prospects of increases in value, or a small income now hoping that the capital will grow? Perhaps the answer lies between these two extremes. Is the money your own, or for your children? Do you pay income tax, and are you likely to worry if your shares fall?

Buying ordinary shares, or equities involves risks. In our example the price went steadily up. It can as easily fall. Your money, your capital is at greater risk in the ordinary share market than in a bank account or debenture. Stocks and shares are not for the man without savings. Some money must be readily available in addition to a home of your own or on mortgage, and enough in reserve to meet the sudden cost of a new car or the expenses of moving house. Shares are for long term investment. They are most unsuitable for savings that will be wanted in a year or two. Selling when all share prices are depressed can lead to large losses. Shares bought with proper advice, to be held for five or more years, should show a steady profit.

We have seen that the cost of buying and selling shares is

substantial. Shares can be bought through your bank, in which case there is no extra to pay, or from a stockbroker. The Stock Exchange will send a list of stockbrokers who are prepared to receive orders from the public. Some are no longer interested in small orders. They are paid on a percentage commission and there is not much more work on a £30,000 order than on a £300 one, although the rewards are much higher.

Savings accounts, bonds and debentures provide a safe income; capital falls with time, eroded by inflation. Shares are a substitute; their value should increase as they represent the real value of property, plant and goods. On the other hand there are risks in ordinary share investment.

The Investment Trust

One answer is the investment trust. It is foolhardy for the new share investor to put all his money into one or two shares. He should aim for at least ten different companies in as many different fields. Since it hardly pays to invest less than £300 in a single company, £3,000 is needed to start. Investment trusts own shares in companies, spreading the risk, and allowing you in one investment of £300 to take part in this spread of investment.

Investment trusts are not really trusts. They are companies whose business is the buying and selling of shares. Some of the money will be in equities, some in debentures and some even in mortgages and other investments outside the Stock Exchange. All the income is pooled together. After management expenses the balance remaining belongs to the shareholders. Some companies issue debentures and preference shares as well as equity capital. This means that after paying off the fixed interest, all the remaining money is paid out as an ordinary dividend. Several good years will see this dividend rise.

Investment trust shares are bought and sold through the Stock Exchange. They cannot be bought directly from the company. Not so with the *unit trust*, which really is a trust.

The Unit Trust

A large number of investments are bought and they make up the portfolio: these underlying securities form the trust fund. The Trustees, usually a bank or insurance company hold the bonds and certificates purchased by the firm running the unit trust.

An investment trust will have a fixed capital. This could be one million shares, and these will be sold; unless there is a bonus or rights issue this capital remains unchanged. A unit trust deals in units, each representing a share in the trust fund, and new units are created or old ones cancelled to meet the day to day demand.

Unit trusts are dealt with at two prices, one for buyers and one for sellers. These prices include the expenses of buying and selling, and reflect the different bid and offer prices of the shares. No further charges are payable.

Investment trust shares are quoted on the Stock Exchange; the price varies according to those laws of supply and demand. They fluctuate, not necessarily because the investments have moved in price. Rarely will an investment trust's 'break-up' value, the amount that the shares it owns would fetch, be the same as the current selling price. Unit trust prices are calculated each day in accordance with a legal formula. This is based entirely on the current stock exchange value of the investments.

Unit trust management companies meet their expenses by charging a certain fixed percentage of the capital value of the trust each year. This, and any profit they make on the buying back and selling of trust units is their only income.

The Trustees collect all the dividends from the shares in the trust, and these are paid out to all the unit holders normally twice a year. They are paid by warrant, like shares, and income tax is deducted first.

No two unit trusts are quite alike. Some are designed to produce a high income; other trusts ignore dividends and concentrate on capital increases in value. A third trust may steer a middle course, and another will put all its money into investments abroad. There are over 200 different unit trusts to choose from, and most large management companies offer a selection of five or six.

The success of a single unit depends upon the managers' skill. It also relies on fresh money flowing in to match unit trust encashments. There are some special trusts which ignore the ordinary member of the public. They may perhaps have a minimum investment of £2000, or they may be open only to charities or trade unions with special tax rules.

Some trusts do not pay out any interest. All income is re-invested as it is received, building up or accumulating within the trust. Such trusts cut out all the paperwork and costs that little cheques sent twice a year can cause.

It takes about the same time to administer a holding of 100 units as to control one 50 times as large. Many trusts encourage the economical large purchaser with a special discount off their normal selling price. Another alternative is to ask unit trust investors to open savings accounts. A fixed sum is paid in, each month, by bankers or giro standing order. Not only does the total saved mount up but also the saver shares in the advantages of 'averaging'. This is the principle that when the unit trust price is low, a fixed sum will buy more units than when the price is high. A £5 monthly payment will purchase more units when the price is depressed, and they benefit accordingly when the price recovers.

Savings schemes have been modified to offer life assurance. The great attraction here is the income tax concession on assurance policies. Some schemes even allow the capital sum to be paid over in units. This could be important if the stock market prices were low when the assurance policy became due.

The Stock Exchange provides the public with a market of stocks and shares to the value of over one hundred thousand million pounds. There they can be exchanged, so that those who wish to invest their money can buy, and those who wish to have their money free again can sell. It gives governments the facilities and the machinery necessary for raising large loans to meet the costs of social welfare, and all the needs of a modern complex state. It allows industry to raise the capital it needs for development and research, and for expansion at home and overseas. Most of British Industry and Commerce is carried on by firms financed by investment through the Stock Exchange.

Be it stocks and shares, or unit trusts, the Stock Exchange provides the apparatus for dealing in them. Unit trusts are easy to buy, easy to sell. Their price varies in the short term, from day to day, although over the years the movement has been ever upwards. They are the bridge between deposit savings, and share ownership. Shares are one of the few forms of investment which consistently have withstood the fall in money value, as prices rise.

THINGS TO DO

1 How much will it cost to invest in shares costing £500? These rise in value to £550 and are then sold. What is your total profit or loss, on the transaction, ignoring tax, but including all expenses and commissions?

2 The London Stock Exchange has two forms of members, jobbers and stockbrokers. Discuss the advantages and disadvantages of this system compared with the common pattern elsewhere of an exchange member who buys and sells with other members directly.

3 Borrow or send off for a copy of the Annual Accounts of any large public company. On most days of the year there will be an advertisement for a company which has just published its accounts, in *The Times* or *The Financial Times* and an address to write to. Study the capital structure (debentures, loan stock and shares), and see how it compares with the total money value of the business.

4 Follow five different shares for five weeks. Choose one in each of the fields—engineering, finance, stores, entertainment and investment trusts. Note how the prices change from day to day. What conclusions do you draw?

5 What is a financial index? Plot the daily progress of one such index over a few months.

6 'Investment is vital to the finance of industry, commerce and Government itself. The Stock Exchange makes invest-

ment possible '. Discuss this statement, and suggest avenues for improvement and change.

7 Follow the fortune of five or six different unit trusts for six weeks. They will be quoted in the daily paper. Watch the difference between the bid and offer prices, and calculate the percentage difference between them.

8 List the main differences between investment trusts and unit trusts.

9 Consider each of the following people carefully. Are unit trusts a suitable investment for them? (a) A man with no savings. (b) A young girl, still single with a steady job. (c) A man aged 25 who knows he will want the money in exactly three years time. (d) A middle-aged couple who have almost paid for their house, and whose children have just left home.

10 You win £25,000, a premium bond prize. Discuss how you would invest this amount in stocks and shares, or unit trusts.

Chapter Eight

The Nation's Budget

The Budget

It is spring in the City of Westminster. Let us go into the Houses of Parliament, and along to the visitors' gallery of the House of Commons. It is packed tight, as is the chamber below. The Speaker has concluded the opening business of the session, and is now leaving although it is only just after 3 pm in the afternoon. Instead the House of Commons becomes a 'Committee of Ways and Means' under its Chairman who sits not in the Speaker's Chair but at the Table. To-day is no ordinary day in the life of Parliament. Today is Budget Day, important to the country and to members alike.

The Chancellor of the Exchequer, the Government's money man, presents his Budget. He does not simply reel off the changes in taxation but in detail explains the Government's policies and aims. He is delivering an account of the steward-ship of the Government for the past twelve months and the financial plans in the year ahead. He is, in his Budget Speech, explaining how and why taxes are to be raised and in turn how they will be spent.

The Nation's Budget is similar to your personal budget. It must take into account where the money is coming from and where it will be going to. No Government, no Chancellor can just add taxes upon taxes, or there would soon be a revolt from the public that has to pay them. At best, when the next election comes round there would be a change in party. At the worst, as happens abroad from time to time, and as has hap-pened in Great Britain in the past, there will be more violent and swifter upsets in the ruling party.

Taxation is imposed to pay for the services and duties of Government and for the administration of the many areas

Budget 1967

Taxes on income **45%**
(including taxes
paid by companies)

Taxes on capital **3%**

**Taxes on
Spending** **33%**

Other receipts **19%**
(including S.E.T.)

**Revenue to be raised
£11,704,000,000**

**Social and
Community
Services** **37%**

How it will be spent

Defence **20%**

Economic services **13%**

National debt **12%**

Miscellaneous **13%**
(including S.E.T. refunds)

Surplus **5%**

where the nation looks after its inhabitants. Each government department will have estimated how much they expect to spend in the coming year. Some of this is already known, while new works will have been costed, and the calculations made. The Ministry of Education will know how much they are prepared to release to build new schools, and they will have also estimated how much will be needed by local councils to pay teachers' wages. The National Health Service, the cost of Social Security, the Armed Forces and the Civil Service will all be spending money, your money, as their part of the work for which the Government is responsible.

No two people will ever agree on exactly how this money should be obtained or how it should be spent. The Government will have a majority in the House of Commons, so eventually their main proposals will be carried. Before they are, the Opposition will attack all points they do not like and there may be discontent from other members. Taxation is unpopular however it is managed. This is big money. In 1865 the National Budget was just over £50 million in expenditure. Today it is over two hundred times as great.

In the Middle Ages the King was expected to live from the money that his own feudal lands produced. In times of war this was nowhere near enough, and taxes were imposed. The history of England and later the United Kingdom is full of quarrels between the King and his subjects about who had the right to levy tax. This was one of the causes of the Civil War, but it was not until the Bill of Rights, passed in 1688 that it was proclaimed that no one should be ' compelled to make any gift, loan, benevolence or tax without common consent by Act of Parliament '. From the earliest days Parliament has concerned itself in money matters. The House of Lords lost the right to change ' Money Bills ' as late as this century.

Today the Government gets its money in three ways—by taxation, from trading profit and through borrowing. We have already touched upon the borrowing side, and remember that it is not just the Government Bonds which make up the loan bill —all National Savings including premium bonds are part of the borrowing force. Nationalised industries contribute something to the credit side. These are the organisations run for us, by us, and their profit comes to us. Not all the state-owned firms make money, but when they do the nation profits.

Taxation

Taxation can be divided into two main sections—direct and indirect. Indirect taxes effect spending, while direct taxation is placed on income and capital. Direct taxation is more important, and indeed is more popular with Chancellors. They can control quite keenly who should pay tax, and how much, so ensuring that the more wealth a man has, the more he pays. Indirect taxation, on goods in the shops, affects everyone, and it can mean that the least well off are forced to pay taxes. No Government really wants to collect from the poor.

Indirect taxation includes purchase tax, originally designed as a check on luxury spending during the Second World War. It was imposed on non-essentials; if the people insisted on buying luxury goods despite the war, then they would have to pay dearly for them. Like all taxes which produce a lot of income, they have remained although the reason originally given has long since gone. Today purchase tax includes goods that were never taxed during the war such as sweets and soft drinks, and the net has spread even wider to include essentials as well as fur coats. Customs and Excise Duties are placed on tobacco and alcoholic drinks at such staggering levels that over 80 per cent of the retail price is made up in tax. Purchase tax is graduated at different percentages according to the type of articles although much less than excise duties. Customs duties are levied on many imported goods, and are the oldest of taxes. Duties were the only source of national income at one time.

Indirect taxation has one advantage to the Government. Once the fuss following its introduction has died down it is paid almost without complaint. The public soon forgets that the tax is there. Licence fees, like the Road Fund Licence to operate a car, and stamp duties on the transfer of stocks, shares or property add up to a fair sum over a year.

Income Tax

It is however direct taxation which has become more important. Income Tax is a levy on everyone's earnings. It was invented in 1799 as a temporary means of raising funds to help pay for the war against Napoleon. It proved so useful, it was renewed again and again until the nation could not afford to run without it. It is now so complicated that accountants charge high fees for sorting out the taxation affairs of their clients. Luckily it is not quite so difficult for the average wage earner.

Everyone who has any income from any source is liable to pay income tax. There are a number of concessions which exempt the very low wage earners, and students still at school who work part-time for a few hours each week. At one end of the scale those on the lowest wages are not asked to pay any income tax at all, and when they do begin to pay the proportion of their total earnings taken remains small. Better-off people pay more, and in addition a greater fraction of their total earnings is taken in tax.

Income tax can vary from year to year. One of the main talking points at budget time is if the Chancellor will reduce the income tax rate, or more gloomily, will he add to it. Changing the rate of tax in the pound brings much work to the Inland Revenue, the Government department responsible for administering these taxes. A less drastic way of altering the total amount of tax that you or I must pay, is to change either the rate or the scope of the many tax allowances. These allowances permit you to keep some of your money without paying any tax on it.

Everyone is entitled to at least one of these ' personal allowances '. The number and size of these allowances depends upon whether you are single or married, how many children are still at home and have not yet started work, and if there are any elderly or infirm relatives whom you support.

The tax law distinguishes between the money you earn, and any cash you receive in interest, dividends and rents. All income that is earned qualifies for an extra ' Earned Income Allowance ', a fixed fraction of total earnings. This fraction can also be changed from year to year.

When all allowances have been calculated, the remainder of your income is subject to tax, at a fixed percentage in each pound. Although each of these pounds is paying tax at say 40 per cent, the actual proportion is much lower over the whole of one's income because the first few hundred pounds, thanks to the allowances, are tax free. The first few hundred pounds always miss the tax; this is why small earners pay none at all.

Most employees pay their tax through ' Pay-as-you-earn ' (PAYE). Calculations including allowances, carried out by the income tax authorities give everyone in employment a code number. This figure is sent to your employer, who with the help of special tables knows how much tax to deduct from your wages each week. The firm must carry out this tax deduction service free of charge, and employ staff to do it. Little wonder then that they call themselves unpaid tax collectors.

Code numbers should take into account every factor known to the tax office. The tables automatically allow for wages if they change because of overtime or promotion, but they do not know when your personal circumstances, and therefore your personal allowances, change. Only if you keep your local tax office, whose address can be obtained from your wages section, fully informed, can you be sure that your code number is correct.

Other deductions worth remembering, which you will only receive if you claim them, include life assurance which has already been mentioned. Superannuation or pension payments are free of tax, and they should be allowed for in your code number. Each year you should receive from your tax office a copy of ' The Notice of Coding ' form. This will state your tax code number, and all tax allowances and their amounts to which the Inspector of Taxes thinks that you are due. Should your pension payments change during the year, for instance after a pay rise, the tax office will not know. If they are not told of the total you have paid they will never know and you could pay too much tax.

Special clothing that is necessarily worn at work is given some relief. You cannot claim what this clothing costs, but instead are given an amount which is supposed to cover the cost of replacement, cleaning and repair. Trades unions, and professional societies charge subscriptions. Much of this expenditure can earn relief. There are other reductions of a specialist nature which you will only receive if you claim. This can be rather difficult if you do not know such allowances exist, so it is well worth while asking your friends at work to see what they have been given. It has been stated that over half the population pays too much tax. Mostly it is a case of small amounts and many are ignorant that there is anything to reclaim.

Working for oneself, there is no PAYE. Members of Parliament, journalists and barrow boys, pop groups and authors are either self-employed, or their wages are called fees. They must tell the tax man what they earn, claim their own allowances, and pay tax in two instalments for the whole year. What is earned in one tax year is not due for payment until the following year, and this can be difficult if the money has all been spent. One often reads of artists and actors who are unable to pay the income tax bill when it is due. They spent the money a year or more before.

Most self-employed people have to call upon accountants to sort out their tax situation; it is so complicated. At least they will find that they can claim for many expenses that the employed worker cannot get; the proof is not so strict.

Other Taxes

Income tax is one way the Government collects its money, but only one. We have mentioned the National Insurance stamp which appears on pay packet deductions; this goes towards many social services which will be dealt with in detail. Other direct taxes include Sur-tax—a kind of income tax paid by people who earn really big incomes; Capital gains tax—levied on the increase in the value of certain goods; Estate Duty—which affects the money we leave, and Corporation tax—a company's income tax.

Capital Gains tax affects the investor in stocks and shares. All increases in value, over and above the original cost is taxable. There are exemptions for small amounts, and you can set off any losses that you suffer but otherwise all gains get taxed. So for that matter does any other substantial item including property which rises in value. Everyone is allowed to have one home which is capital tax free. Otherwise all increases are taxable.

Estate Duty is payable on death. Small estates at first sight appear to receive a generous exemption from duty, but this limit allows for only a modest house and an insurance policy. All extra money above the exemption limit left on death is charged at a percentage which rises steeply. This includes the value of all property, collections, stocks and shares and everything that can be turned into money. Estate Duties are high, and are an example of the nation claiming its share of wealth that was not otherwise taxed during the life of the owner.

National Insurance

The Weekly National Insurance contribution is a perfect example of a tax. The dictionary defines tax as ' A compulsory contribution levied on persons, property or businesses to meet the expenses of government or other public service '.

Everybody pays National Insurance contributions unless they are too young or too old. This is a flat rate tax, with different charges made on those at work under 18, and between men and women. Your employer will pay an extra amount for you, and the rest of his staff. When you are not at work, or should you start your own business then there is a new scale of charges; these are paid each week by means of special stamps bought at the post office.

You must belong to the National Insurance Scheme. It provides weekly flat-rate benefits during sickness and unemployment, and there are other payments to widows, orphans, and during maternity or death.

Your actual weekly payment depends upon your employer. If he is ' contracted out ', this means that he has promised to pay a pension at least as good as the largest state pension. If not, then both you and he pay an extra sum towards a graduated pension, based on the amount of your earnings. This graduated pension is added on to the flat-rate state pension.

Your weekly stamp goes towards a variety of schemes. Best known is the National Health Service; there is also the Industrial Injuries which looks after anyone injured during work. Employers pay extra amounts towards Redundancy Payments, and the Selective Employment Tax.

If you are at work for more than a few hours each week you must pay for your stamp. If you are over 18 and below retirement age, 65 for men and 60 for women, then you must pay even if you are not at work. The only exceptions are certain married women whose husbands pay. When you are sick or unemployed then the Social Security office will arrange to 'credit' your weekly stamp. If you do not pay for any other reason, perhaps for instance you are still at college, then your benefits will not be earned and your final state pension will be lower.

Sickness benefit tends to be the one Social Security payment that most people will receive sooner or later. This is a flat sum, with extra for a wife and children. You do not get this automatically; to receive the full rate you must have paid or had credited 50 out of 52 contributions in the previous year. To claim, a medical certificate is sent to the Social Security Office, and this must be done within six days of falling sick.

Unemployment benefit is paid under the same sort of rules as sickness; you can receive it for one year, but there are ways to lose it. You must take any reasonable job that is found for you, and you cannot receive this allowance while on strike.

The minimum retirement age for men is 65 and for women 60. At this age they qualify for the state retirement pension, although there is no need to take it. Instead anyone may go on working for another five years earning a larger amount. After that the pension is yours even if you remain at work. Retirement according to the Social Security Office means that you have either given up all paid work or most of it. A small amount may be earned each week—it really is minute—and if you receive more, then the pension is reduced or stopped altogether.

Pensions are made up of four parts: (a) flat rate (b) additions for dependants (c) graduated pension (d) a supplement for carrying on beyond the earliest retirement age. Graduated pensions are paid out of earnings unless your firm itself offers you a good retirement scheme. Then you may be ' contracted-out ', and the firm promises to make up the pension to at least as much as the state would have paid. You only earn a full pension if you have paid on average, 50 contributions each year from 18 to retirement. University students will often fail to reach this figure, and their retirement pension will be affected.

Other benefits which are paid from National Insurance include Widow's benefits, guardians allowance, child's special allowance and death grant. Your Social Security office will explain these in detail.

Social Security
Not everyone qualifies for national insurance benefits yet they can be in real need. The Government thinks that it has a duty to all its citizens, and quite rightly makes some provisions to see that everyone has enough food, fuel and clothing, and that they can pay the rent. Consider a man, whose wife dies, leaving him with three young children to look after. Which is more important to this man—that he goes out to work, letting the local council board out his children at public expense, or that he stays at home, and brings up his family together? Extra benefits are paid to anyone without money and unable to earn. No one need starve today.

Family allowances to families with more than one child under 19, and at least two children not yet at work, help the least well off. Although the family allowance is payable to all families, those that earn too much will find that they pay it all back again in tax.

The National Health Service offers medical, hospital, dental and other services, and is available to all. It is financed partly by the health contribution in the weekly stamp. About one-ninth of the total cost comes from you directly—the rest is paid out of other taxation.

The Redundancy Payments Act sees that if you lose your job which you have held for more than two years, because the firm no longer needs anyone to do your work, then you will be compensated.

Social Security is not new. Concern and compassion has often been shown for those in need and the aged. What is modern in concept and design is the Welfare State. Benefits are not free, and they are not charity. They are the right of everyone paid for by the nation as a whole out of their taxation to those who are less fortunate.

Income tax and social security are examples of how the Government takes away and how it pays back. Taxes on spending and capital makes up most of its remaining income; payments on other community services, defence, economic services and the national debt account for most of the expenditure. The National Debt, which is the money we owe ourselves, has grown large because when the Government thinks that taxation has gone far enough it borrows. The amount that it now owes in stocks is so great that over one tenth of its expenses each year is the payment of interest on loans. In part this is the legacy of two world wars. More important it is a reflection of the increasing amount spent on the citizens by their government.

You will no doubt hear older people sigh for a return to the days when there was less taxation. They forget that today governments spend more on social services. Education has expanded, and the school leaving age has risen. Today everyone has better facilities while at school, and more is spent on each student. After school, according to their interests, there are universities, polytechnics, night schools, day release colleges, colleges of education and further education on a scale undreamed of fifty years ago. Facilities mean money, and the only person who can pay is you the tax payer.

THINGS TO DO

1 Calculate your family's personal allowance for the year. With these allowances calculate the amount of tax that you would have to pay on a gross wage of (a) £1000, (b) £2000 per year. In each case work out the proportion of the total wages that goes in tax.

2 Discuss how income tax is imposed, calculated and paid. How would you improve the system?

3 'Income tax is unfair to the richest and poorest sections of the community.' Is this true? Discuss this statement.

4 Income tax could be abolished if all the revenue was transferred to the goods we buy in the form of a sales tax. Do you think that this would be a good idea?

5 Families with very small incomes sometimes find that their tax allowances are more than they earn. They do not pay any income tax. Is this social justice?

6 Compare the Society Security scene as it was before 1939 and as it is now.

7 Make out a table of the different rates of social security benefits, and the national insurance stamps for different types of worker.

8 It is sometimes said that the trouble with government benefits is that they are paid regardless of need. Do you agree? What would you do to change the situation?

9 What problems arise when the government tries to look after the less fortunate sections of the community? What problems face the less fortunate, when they try to make ends meet?

10 If you had the power, what form of taxation would you abolish or reduce? To balance the Budget what would you put in its place?

11 What are the current rates of purchase tax, and what are the broad categories of goods that are covered by each rate?

12 How is the Government's income spent during one year?

13 What is the National Debt? How can it be reduced?

Your Local Council

Members of a family sometimes join together to pay expenses. Three or four children pool their money to buy an expensive birthday present; two sisters agree to share the cost of keeping a kitten or puppy. On a larger scale, this is what councils do within a neighbourhood.

Services provided to our families are expensive, and we would have to do without them if they were not organised by the local council. Water to wash in and drink, drains and sewers to take the waste away. Roads kept clean and in good repair, policemen preserving law and order. These are some of the services that your local council either runs itself or helps other bodies to provide.

Services fall into three main categories. First there are those which keep you well, such as piped clean water, and the sewerage system. The dustmen who take away your rubbish and dispose of it safely, and the men who clean the streets and repair them are protecting the health of your family as much as the council clinic which gives advice to young mothers. Second there are the services which protect your life and home: police, fire and ambulance are provided either by your own council or by a special body which your council has joined. Third there are the services which make life so much more rewarding and enjoyable. Parks and swimming baths, museums and libraries, council houses and schools; these services and many others are needed in the neighbourhood; the people living there must pay for them.

The National Government does not want to control every detail of people's life and welfare. Long ago they decided that many parts of government could best be organised on a district basis to fit in with local needs.

The Central Government has delegated certain tasks to local authorities, and also sees that they do them properly. This local authority or council is made up of councillors, elected by the people in the area. They are helped in their duties by a team of paid officials, from the town clerk to librarians. Councillors are not paid, and they give up much of their time to the people they serve. Apart from council meetings, there are committees which meet and look at the detailed problems. These committees concentrate on one aspect of the council's work—for instance parks and recreation grounds.

Each committee fights to get money for the services they want to provide. If everyone got everything they asked for, there would soon be a massive bill to pay, so a Finance Committee looks at all the proposals, and divides out the funds that are available. The Finance Committee looks after the people's money, and sees that none is wasted. You vote for your councillor, who with his fellow councillors makes up the council. Local authorities give their committees the power to work out details, and employ paid officials to carry them out. These benefits affect you and your family, who elected the council in the first place, and pay the cost now.

It is one thing to decide that you want to spend money. It is another to find all that is needed. A local council will divide its costs into two sections, capital expenditure and current expenditure.

Capital expenditure covers money that is spent on items of long lasting value : Schools and libraries, old people's homes and new roads. The council may borrow this money either from companies with spare cash, or from anyone who is willing to lend. Local council bonds pay higher rates of interest than ordinary savings accounts and are quite safe. The interest, and the money to repay the loans is found by the people who live in the area. Sometimes with expensive projects the Government at Westminster will help and make either an interest-free loan or an outright grant or gift.

Current expenditure can be covered by Government grants

and it may also be earned by the council. Rents on council houses, fines on library books, rent on football pitches and admission to tennis courts or swimming baths are some of the ways the money comes in. It amounts to a sizeable sum in an enterprising local council area, but it is still by no means enough. The remainder and bulk of income has to be found through rates.

Rates

Rates are a local tax. This tax or ' rate ' is paid by everyone who occupies any property in the neighbourhood, and as we must all live somewhere, we all pay our local rate to the council either directly or through rent indirectly.

Every piece of land, every building in the country has been assessed at a nominal figure known as the rateable value. In theory this is the rent which could be expected if the building was available to be let, but in practice this precise meaning has become distorted. Every house is seen and its value is calculated. At one time, Government valuers were supposed to bring the rateable value up to date every five years, but the intervals are longer today. A house with a rateable value of £150 is probably supposed to fetch £250 in rent, and £100 has been deducted from the higher figure as a repair allowance. It is probable that this house would fetch considerably more if it was offered to let.

The better the house, the higher the rateable value and this can upset proud householders who have exerted time and energy on their property, improving facilities. Additions like garages or central heating make the rateable value rise, presumably because the rent that could be asked has also increased.

Shops, factories, office blocks, farms and woodlands are all rated, and each is liable for its contribution towards the cost of local government. Heavy industry, towering office blocks and extensive factories are very highly rated indeed.

All the rateable values are added together, and the total in the council area is calculated. In a large borough the total value of property could well run beyond one million pounds.

Take as an example the imaginary London Borough of New-chester with a property rateable value of exactly £1,000,000. The council knows from past experience the running costs of its services, including staff, maintenance and replacements. New works and services will have been costed. Apart from its own budget, the Greater London Council will have sent in its bill for the services that it provides to the whole area, and there will be a similar account from the Metropolitan Police. To simplify figures, suppose that all expenses under all headings total £600,000. Then for each pound of property value, 60p must be collected. The council declares a rate of 60p in the pound, and this is where the name ' rates ' comes from.

Rates are a form of tax, levied not on how much money you have, but on the type of property that you live in. It is a property tax. Many people think that it is out of date as the way to pay for local council services. They give as an example two houses, exactly the same, next door to each other. In one house there are four wage earners, a married couple and two grown up children with a total wage of £120 each week. In the identical house next door a family of four, but the children are still young. Only the husband can go to work, and he brings home £30 each week. Both households hold four people, both pay the same amount in rates yet one house has an income four times as great as the other.

Each council prepares a bill for the rate due, giving a complete breakdown of how the money will be used. In Newchester they explain that each penny produces £10,000, and then go into detail showing how the rate of 60p in the pound is made up. It looks like this:

STATEMENT OF RATE SERVICES

Purposes	Amount of rate in pence in the pound		
	Borough	G.L.C.	Police
Ambulance services		1.00	
Baths and washhouses	.55		
Cemeteries and Crematoria	.54		
Children's services	5.97		
Cleansing of streets	1.88		
Education		38.97	
Fire Service		1.78	
Health services	11.10		
Highways	5.09	1.88	
Housing	16.45	6.04	
Libraries and museums	2.22	.02	
Parks and open spaces	.77	1.21	
Police			18.67
Magistrates' Courts			.77
Probation system			.46
Public Lighting	.95		
Removal of house refuse	4.44	1.15	
Sewerage and drainage	1.25	2.36	
Social services—aged persons	7.75		
Town planning	1.98	1.67	
Contingencies	1.00	.48	
Other services and expenses	1.87	1.66	
GROSS TOTALS	63.81	58.22	19.90
Subsidies, and other government grants	11.41	5.32	10.10
Rate support grant	30.40	24.70	
TOTAL DEDUCTIONS	41.81	30.02	10.10
NET RATE	22.00	28.20	9.80

Summary

Borough purposes	—	22.00
Greater London	—	28.20
Metropolitan police	—	9.80
TOTAL		60.00

Rates Calculations

This balance sheet may confuse you with its two places of decimals. This is not the fault of the council. They are explaining why they need the money, and where is goes, so that you may be kept informed. The council represents you; they believe that you have the right to know how they will be spending your money.

Let us simplify the statement, by imagining that your house has a rateable value of exactly £200. At 60p in the pound the rates will total £120 in all, which will be payable in 2 instalments of £60 each, probably in April and October. Many families find that this is too much to find all at once, and they agree to pay in monthly instalments over ten months. The Newchester council allows this, as long as the monthly payments are made by bankers order or giro standing order, and that the payments are consecutive and begin in April. They charge nothing extra for these credit terms of £12 monthly.

What are you getting for £120? As your rateable value is £200, the number of pence spent on any service listed is found by multiplying by 200. Cleaning the streets will cost 1.88p in each pound. Your share will be 200 x 1.88 or 376p, that is

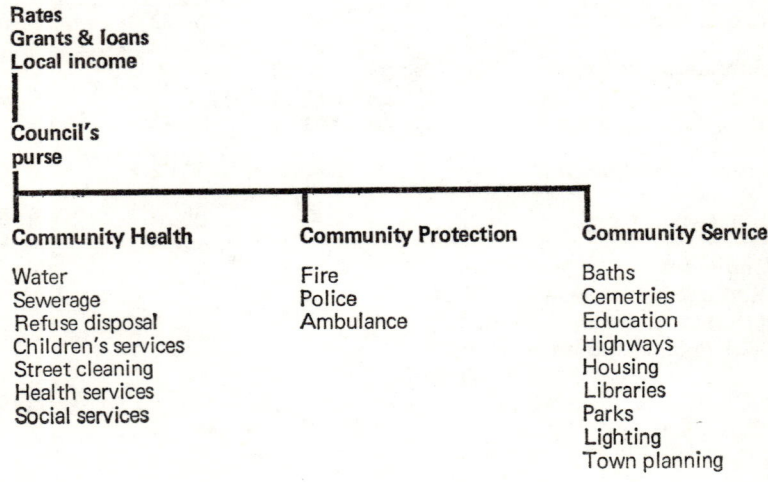

Rates
Grants & loans
Local income

Council's
purse

Community Health	Community Protection	Community Services
Water	Fire	Baths
Sewerage	Police	Cemetries
Refuse disposal	Ambulance	Education
Children's services		Highways
Street cleaning		Housing
Health services		Libraries
Social services		Parks
		Lighting
		Town planning

£3.76. Similarly public lighting comes to £1.90 (200 x .95p) and education reaches a staggering £77.94. Education is the largest single item to appear on the rate demand but there are government grants for many of these services and education receives more than any other. This does not stop householders without children from complaining that they have to pay for services they do not want. The whole idea of a community and a local authority to administer it, is that everyone shares in the expenses of all services, and they use those that they need. Otherwise there would be a cry from every resident that they did not use the swimming baths, or the library or even the police!

Government grants in this particular case totalled 81.93p in every pound, or £163.86 for your home. This helps to keep local taxation down, although as the central Government must find its funds from somewhere, it is possible that you are getting back other taxes of some kind.

Since the mid 1960s private houses, as compared with shops and factories, have had a small reduction in their rates and in Newchester it amounted to 9p in each pound. This reduced the rates to 51p in the pound, or £102 in total; this is still a lot but a worthwhile reduction. Shops and offices and all non-private dwellings do not receive this extra discount.

You will have realised that rates can be expensive, and they are too much for those on a small income. Rebates are now granted to anyone earning only a limited amount. The rate bill if £102 could be reduced to £39 if one was entitled to the full rebate.

Local government is based on the idea that those services which can be run locally are best arranged that way. Local people know the special problems and particular needs. It would be easy to arrange that the fire services were run on a nationwide basis, but there is much to be said in favour of regional operations. This is a compromise, not too large to become impersonal, yet not so small as to be inefficient.

Education is administered on a local basis, county councils and county boroughs running their own schools in their own way. Only in London is there an exception to this rule. There the Inner London boroughs combine to form the Inner London Education Authority. The larger the unit of organisation, the greater will be the streamlining of services with savings in supplies and lower expenses. Small councils may be at some disadvantage over money, although they may be better with the personal touch. In all cases parents have some say in the running of their own education service, and they know where to go, for advice or with complaints. If education was run by the Ministry of Education it is unlikely that parents would be so eager to go to the local office.

Local affairs are run by local councils, elected by people who live in the area. Today councils tend to work along party political lines, with national rather than local affairs the key at election time. Nevertheless councillors will watch local feelings. They are always trying to keep the rates down, while at the same time giving their electorate as wide a range of services to be proud of as possible.

THINGS TO DO

1 Who are your local councillors; what is the name of the ward and the council in the area where you live? When and where do council meetings take place? Where can you read the minutes of the last Council Meeting?

2 Either use the example in the text, or find a recent rate demand at home. Compare the cost of the various services, and work out how much your house pays towards libraries, social services and the police.

3 Display in a diagram the proportion paid to each of the local services.

4 From your local council offices or the library, find out the rate in the pound demanded over the past ten years. Display the information on a graph or chart. If there have been any large changes in the rate, find out why they were made.

5 How would you change your local taxation to make the system fairer? How could the rate system be kept, and still made fairer to families with only one wage earner?

6 In the United States local communities operate a 'sales tax' to pay for community projects. This is a percentage added to all retail sales. Give your own reasons why this system would or would not work in the United Kingdom.

Chapter Ten   Sensible Shopping

Shopping Rights

We spend most of our income in the shops, mainly on food, but also on clothing, household goods and luxuries. Every purchase is a contract between the buyer and the shopkeeper. You cannot go along to a shop and insist that an overcoat in the window is sold to you, or that it is sold at the price on the ticket. Everything on display is an 'invitation to treat'. When you say that you would like that £15 coat, you are replying to such an invitation. There is still no contract, and you could change your mind and leave the shop; it could be that the shopkeeper decides to keep the coat. Neither is likely, but that is the law, and shopkeepers have been known to refuse to disturb their window display. Once the shopkeeper accepts your offer, a contract is made and is binding—either side can now break the contract only if the other agrees.

You as a shopper have rights. Most important is the protection given by the Trade Descriptions Act which came into force on 30 November 1968. This does not allow anyone to make a false or misleading description about the goods offered for sale, or to make false promises about the supply of goods, or to knowingly make false statements about any service, accommodation or facility. Nylon shirts must be made of nylon and an eight ounce steak must not weigh less. If sales goods are offered at 50p reduced from £1, they must have been sold at £1 for at least 28 consecutive days in the previous six months.

If you have a complaint, concerning the way goods are described, you can get in touch with your local Weights and Measures Department at the Town Hall. Dishonest descriptions are unlikely; this act makes any falsehood a criminal offence.

One of the oldest laws which give you rights as a shopper is the Sales of Goods Act 1893. It lists the rules which apply when you buy. If you order by description, such as the wording on a label, order form or from a catalogue, then the goods must be exactly as described. The shopkeeper is not allowed to substitute something of a different quality. If you ask for all-wool socks, then you must not be given a mixture of wool and cotton. Your purchases, bought by description from someone who normally deals in those goods, must be of 'merchantable quality'. A spin dryer that will not spin, a school satchel which falls apart after one week's use—these are not of merchantable quality.

You would expect that whatever you buy, it would be fit for the purpose you had in mind, within reason. There are three conditions: (a) the goods must be of a kind that the shopkeeper normally sells; (b) you let the shopkeeper know why you want the goods, unless it is obvious (it is taken for granted that a chair will be sat on, and that you will want to listen to a radio); (c) you must not ask for the goods by a trade name. If these conditions are broken you will have given up any rights as to their 'fitness for purpose' although you are still protected by 'merchantable quality'.

There are other acts although they generally apply only to food and goods sold by weight.

Types of Shops

Today there are so many different types of shops. Let us take them one by one. The specialist shops are the oldest. These include things like the greengrocer and the baker, the grocer and the ironmonger, the sweet shops. These shops are where you should get expert advice and help. They may be able to give after-sales service, especially with such items as electrical goods. Many will arrange delivery to your home, and accept telephone orders. These are shops where you may be able to obtain credit on an informal, no charges, basis.

These specialist shops are convenient, just around the corner and some stay open late. You will get personal service but they do tend to charge the full price for all they sell. This may mean that their stock remains on the shelves a long time, and that there is not a wide choice of branded goods. It is possible that food shops may be inefficient, with no refrigerated or deep freeze facilities, and food can be wasted. The prices you pay will be greater if a shopkeeper is inefficient and his stock becomes useless.

Departmental stores were for many years very advanced in their method of selling. They offered the personal service of a private shop with a variety of goods that the small man could not hope to keep. They still offer account services, and delivery, but their profit margins have been cut. They no longer show the big profits of thirty years ago, but they have kept their reputations. Should you complain, your case will be carefully and courteously investigated. They continue the advantage of ' one-stop ' shopping.

Multiple and chain stores are to be found on every town and suburban city High Street. They sell goods which range from clothes to shoes, paints to groceries. Multiples are all controlled under one head office, which buys in large quantities, and some of the savings are passed on to the customer. Many multiples specialise in food or clothes, others offer a wide range of goods imitating on a smaller scale the departmental store.

Co-operative stores are a special type of multiple, where the customers become members of the society, and they run the store by voting for their own managing directors. The profits are returned to the customer as a dividend, paid back at so much on each pound of purchases.

You will always find bargains on the barrows of street markets. They are busy, and the reason is that they are much cheaper, Stall holders pay rent, but nothing like the amount a shopkeeper in the same street pays. Their stock is limited; this cuts down the expenses, and regular buyers at established stalls find that they come away satisfied. There is a natural suspicion of market produce, which puts the stall holder on his mettle. It can be a different story if a barrow is here today and not seen again at the market for six months!

Mail-order trading is popular in rural areas, where there is only a limited choice in local shops. Mail-order firms employ different selling methods: from small advertisements to large catalogues. Small advertisements must be backed by 'satisfaction or money back' guarantees, if they are to be accepted by publishers of newspapers and magazines. Mail-order firms spend large sums on advertising and on their catalogues; they could not survive if their stock was not satisfactory. Their products are sent on approval, and they would soon make a loss if much was returned.

Buying in bulk should give you a discount. When you go into a shop, it costs no more to sell you six pounds of tea than a single quarter-pound packet. You might expect a reduction but it is unusual in a local shop. Bulk buying companies allow you to order direct through the mail, and there are worthwhile savings after postage has been met.

There are shops which only allow you to buy there if you hold a club membership card, or some other form of identification. Their goods are on sale at lower than retail prices. Other clubs offer their members discounts at certain shops listed in a membership directory. Cash-and-carry shops provide self service in bulk, charging low prices because there are no service charges to be met.

Most houses still have the milkman calling. This is shop-to-door trading. Other examples are the baker or fishmonger, and in country districts a local supermarket may operate a mobile shop. Credit traders bring a wide range of goods to the door, and allow purchases to be paid for by weekly instalments. The idea is to keep the customers interested in something new, so that they continue the instalments which contain a credit charge.

Shopping Hints

What should you look for when shopping? Although the shopper is not always right, and some can be really unreasonable, shops are there to persuade you to buy; without customers they would close. Prices vary from store to store. There are large department stores which always seem to be more expensive than any other; they are luxurious, their service is without

E

fault, and they make buying a pleasure. Small shops which seem on the point of closing down, everything an untidy mess, charge prices that appear unbeatable. Most shops fall somewhere in between. The type of shop you visit depends upon how much you can afford and the quality you want.

The Consumers' Council gave some hints in its booklet *About Shopping* (regrettably this organisation is no more). When buying household equipment it asked these questions: Will it do the job the customer wants? Who vouches for its performance? Is it the right size? Will it stand up to wear and tear? Who will service it if anything goes wrong? Who pays for the servicing? Does the charge include labour and replacement parts, transport to and from the repair shop? Will it chip, rust, stain, break? Is it safe? Is it easy to keep clean?

Most expensive goods are sold with a ' warranty ' or ' guarantee '. The rights of a customer have already been mentioned in some detail. Many guarantees actually take away more than they give in return. Remember that if the goods do not do the job that they should, and if you relied upon the retailer's skill and advice, then you have, under the Sales of Goods Act, rights against that retailer. Goods must be of reasonable quality and fit for the purpose for which you brought them. If they break down soon afterwards, then the retailer is liable. There are shops where the owner or manager does not like this law, but they have to accept it eventually.

Guarantees, if they are worth having, add to your rights, and do not take any away. The manufacturer should promise to accept all responsibility for the goods. He should agree to repair or replace defective goods free of charge, and this includes packing, postage and labour as well as the cost of spare parts. He should state that he will pay compensation for damage or loss, caused by defects, and that he will conform to all responsibilities imposed by the law. Retailers are still liable, even when there is a guarantee, and you should only accept and sign a warrantry when you are sure that it is in your favour.

It would be unreasonable to expect every single item that a manufacturer makes, to work perfectly. There must be some faulty goods, or inspection costs would send the final price rocketing. If there is a fault, go back to the retailer. He should agree to put defects right, at no cost to you. In theory, if he does not, you could sue him for damages in court, although it is unlikely to go that far. The manufacturer too must share some of the responsibility, and most are reasonable when there are genuine faults. Some complaints are unfair, like the one from a young man who stated that his shoes had fallen to pieces and he had only worn them every day for two years!

If you have a genuine complaint go straight to the top. It is usually a waste of time dealing with sales assistants; they do not have any authority to handle complaints. Ask for the buyer in a departmental store, or the manager in a multiple. The higher you go, the more likely are you to find someone who knows what to do, and has the power to put it right. If you write, be polite. It puts the reader in a good mood, and he will try to meet reason with reason.

If you are still unsatisfied, call in at the Citizens' Advice Bureau—the address can be found in the telephone directory. They will give you help and advice in planning the next step, which could be a letter to the head office, or to the manufacturer. Perhaps there is a trade association or an advisory council which could be approached. If all else fails there is always a solicitor. The Legal Advice Scheme allows you to discuss your problem with a solicitor, for a small fee.

Most appliances last out their guarantee period, and eventually fail through fair wear and tear some years after they have been purchased. They will then need to be serviced. To avoid the need for servicing when it may be inconvenient, for instance if the electric fire or blanket breaks down in midwinter, you should consider how to maintain complicated appliances. Modern electrical and gas equipment can make life easier, but it does create problems when it fails to work properly.

If your electric cooker, or gas poker fails to work, you will want it serviced as quickly as possible. Servicing is provided by the gas and electricity boards; most servicing calls could have been prevented by sensible precautions.

You cannot expect your equipment to be serviced at an exact time during the day. Service engineers leave with a rota of jobs, and they have no idea how long each one will take. On a Monday, it may be impossible to get the engineer to call that day, although it would be unreasonable to wait too long if a refrigerator or deep freeze failed.

Unpleasant surprises are usually caused by the bill. Labour charges seem to consist of excessive amounts, and a typical sarcastic remark is ' I wish that I was paid as much '. This is unfair as the rate per hour will include travelling time, and an allowance for the time the engineer sits in his office waiting for calls. If you give the engineer a cup of tea then do not be surprised if you have to pay for his time while he drinks it, and that could be as much as 50p.

Comparisons

We spend on average between one third and one quarter of our money on food and drink. It is one of the largest items in our personal budget. The more we earn, the more we seem to spend. Although there is a limit to the amount we can hope to consume, improved quality, new foodstuffs and exotic luxuries can be bought, if more money is available.

It is easy enough to compare prices of the same foodstuffs in different shops; sometimes one has to be a mathematical genius to compare prices of different size packages. Many large stores make special offers which remain on sale at low prices for a week or two; they then revert to the regular rate. These offers can be made to tempt you inside the store, where they hope that you will buy something else. Much of a shop's profit comes from ' impulse buying ' of this type. Special offers may introduce a new brand or an entirely new food. Canned rice pudding, and instant mashed potato are two food lines introduced into the shops in this way.

No food is a bargain unless it is fresh. A shop is supposed to make sure that the food it sells is not stale, and that it returns unsold perishable manufactured foods to the makers. Occasionally, stock control fails and out-of-date food is sold by mistake. Learn the code at your local shop or supermarket which tells you when food was packed. Make sure that the frozen foods they sell have not been thawed and refrozen—

although this is difficult. Canned goods may be dented—if the top of the can pops backwards and forwards it has probably 'blown' and it not worth buying.

Know your way around the different foodstuffs. There are six grades of liquid milk, and many more lines of cream. Your milkman may sell three different types of milk and your grocer can possibly supply three to four varieties of cream. Meat is a subject in itself; in general the cheaper cuts of meat cost less because they take longer to prepare for cooking, or they contain a lot of bone. Expensive cuts of meat, like chops and steaks, can be cooked quickly; they are popular with families when everyone is out all day. Demand forces the price up.

Shopping is not difficult, but do not try to do it in a hurry. Shop around, comparing prices and qualities whenever you have the time. Choose carefully, making sure that what you buy is what you want. If it fails to please, do not be afraid to return to the shop, and explain what has happened. In ninety-nine cases out of one hundred you will find that either all is well, or the goods are replaced. For the odd one that is faulty, and the shop refuses to listen, then you can write to the manufacturer or the head office of the firm that sold it to you. If all else fails, it is possible to sue for the value of the goods in court, although this is a remote possibility. Sensible shoppers should have no problems.

THINGS TO DO

1 Make a map of your High Street. Mark on the map the type of shops, for example, department store, multiple, specialist, and so on.

2 Look at three or four different guarantee forms, from different makers. Which of these gives the best repair or replacement promise to the shopper?

3 Visit your local Citizens' Advice Bureau, and ask them how they can help the shopper.

4 Sensible shoppers will have few problems. How is it possible to prevent difficulties arising at all?

5 Most electrical goods will fail sometimes. In many cases

it is because the plug wiring has a bad connection. Explain how to wire a plug (three pin) correctly.

6 Choose five different electrical appliances. List what you would do, in the home, to keep them well maintained.

7 Compare meat prices at two butchers' shops for five or six different cuts of beef or lamb.

8 Eggs are sold at different prices for different sizes. What do these sizes represent? Why do some shops charge more for brown shelled eggs? What are ' free range ' eggs, and why do they cost more?

9 Look at the packaging of any foodstuffs in the larder. Some will have a long list of contents. Does the order of contents of a made-up foodstuff signify anything? What would you want to know about a particular brand of stewing steak or tinned fruit?

10 Your television set has stopped working. What would you do before you ring up the service engineers? What would you tell the servicing firm on the telephone?

Chapter Eleven Running a Car

Buying a Car

A motor car is part of the modern scene, an essential feature of life today rather than a luxury. In a town it can be a time saver when there is a difficult cross-city journey to be made. In country districts it is essential as public transport is reduced and withdrawn.

Cars are not cheap to buy. They are expensive to run. Before we list the many expenses that make up the running costs of a car, we will look at a few of the buying problems. The maker will recommend a selling price for new cars. This figure usually applies only to a basic model. Extras which many motorists consider essential can send the price up. Second-hand cars are usually accepted as they stand. There will be repairs and a few additions to be installed before the enthusiastic new owner is satisfied. In either case, the vehicle will then be ready to take away.

CAR COSTS

Allowances For	*Licences*
Dealer's Profit	**Driving**
Depreciation	**Road Traffic Act**
Repairs	**Test Certificate**
Maintenance	**Insurance**
Running Costs	**Organisation Membership**
Oil and Petrol	*Overheads*
Car Cleaning	**Garage Rent**
Parking Fees	**Tool Kit**
Fines and Penalties	

There is a choice to be made between a new car and a second-hand one. Which you choose will depend upon the amount of money available and the way that you like to buy— cash down or through some form of credit agreement. It will also turn on the way in which the car will be used. This can vary from the straightforward half hour jog each day, to the extensive mileage involved in the journeys of a commercial traveller on the road all the week.

New cars are normally sold at the standard prices recommended by the manufacturers. Used cars are a matter of bargaining. Rarely will a used-car buyer expect to pay the price quoted by the dealer; both sides expect some hard bargaining to a more acceptable level.

Most cars are bought from garages, and both new and second-hand models may be obtained in part-exchange. An old vehicle will be accepted by the garage in part settlement of the bill when another car is bought. The amount offered by a dealer will depend as much on how easy your old car is to sell, as on the profit he knows he has made on the new one you are buying. You can usually be sure that you will be offered more for a car in part-exchange than in a straightforward, no-strings-attached sale.

It is always possible to buy privately and sell privately. There are a number of dodges in the car selling game, some sailing rather close to the wind, and others outright dishonest. A small advertisement in the evening newspaper, with telephone number could well lead to a kiosk, where the seller is waiting for a victim to call. The car is brought round for inspection, priced rather less than such a car should be, and in its immaculate condition is snapped up as a bargain. Four weeks later it turns out to be a stolen vehicle. The car goes back to its rightful owner, and you may claim back the money you handed over to the seller. Unfortunately he cannot be traced from his telephone kiosk number, so you have little chance of seeing your money again.

Private sales are usually for cash. A dealer will be able to arrange credit terms; if a car salesman can be sure that you need hire-purchase or some other form of loan, then he may be willing to reduce his asking price even further. He will more than make up for any cash lost by his commission from the credit firm or finance house. Once papers have been signed, accepting the loan, the credit contract is between you and the finance company—the dealer is no longer involved. Interest rates for credit to arrange the purchase of motor vehicles are high. These credit charges must be included in the cost of a car.

You have bought the car of your dreams, or at least as near to it as you can afford. The hire-purchase forms are signed up, the deposit has been paid, and you are impatient to be on the road. Before you can drive away there are four further formalities to be concluded, and each of them will be an added item of expense.

Insurance and Other Overheads

Most second-hand cars require a Ministry of Transport Test certificate, and although your used car will probably be covered, the older and shakier cars get, the less likely that they have passed the test. You must hold a driving licence. All mechanical vehicles except for motor cycles and a few others, can only be driven by owners of a full driving licence, unless there is a qualified driver present. These two documents are quite cheap. More expensive is the Motor Vehicle licence although there is a reduction for the full year. Finally the Road Traffic Act makes it compulsory for every vehicle to be covered by a valid insurance policy that protects the public. Identical insurance policies cost differing amounts according to the area where the car will be used, the age and experience of the driver.

Insurance can be expensive and the most costly form is known as a comprehensive policy. Although it gives most protection it does not safeguard a driver against every possible expense. What a typical policy will do is to pay all costs arising from death or injury to third parties. You and the insurance company are the first and second parties of an insurance contract. Everyone else, passengers and pedestrians and other road users are third parties. A comprehensive cover will also include loss or damage to your car by fire accident or theft, and the payment of all legal costs.

Extra benefits available under most schemes include personal accident cover, with payments for loss of limbs or sight, foreign travel, medical expenses and accommodation if the car is badly damaged and cannot be driven.

A policy is valid only if you hold a driving licence. You are expected to use the vehicle in the way that you stated you would on the application form. Do not expect an insurance company to pay if a car is used all the time as a mini-cab, and you stated that it would only be driven for pleasure. All the statements on the application form must be true, and this includes experience, age and your driving record.

Some things are excluded. Wear and tear, mechanical breakdowns, and loss of use. This last item could be important, and costly if you have to hire a car to carry on your work. If the accident is your fault then you will have to meet the bill yourself; if the blame falls on another driver you should be able to claim back from his insurance company.

A motorist can earn a bad record, either by appearing too often in a police court, or by experiencing a long list of bad accidents with heavy claims. Some cars are more risky than others. Sports cars are more difficult to insure. Cars kept in the street rather than in a private yard or garage are more likely to be broken into or damaged by hooligans. These are the type of circumstances which may force an insurance company to say that the risk is unacceptable. They will probably ask for a larger premium each year, and in addition they may expect you to pay the first few pounds of every claim. Sometimes they will even restrict your driving each year to a given number of miles. Restrictions, and payments towards each claim can also be agreed to voluntarily, bringing down the actual cost.

A ' third party cover ' looks after exactly what it says. It will pay for all claims by third parties, but none of the expenses that you yourself incur. One alternative is to add fire and theft loss, so that if these happen you will be paid. Finally there is a ' Road Traffic Act Policy ', covering only what the law insists must be insured. Any other accident or incident will not be paid for by the company. A few unlucky or bad drivers can only buy this type of protection. Average motorists can buy this form of cover very cheaply; it covers so little that it really is dear for what you get, and would still be too much at even half the premium.

Insurance companies are in competition with each other. No two firms will offer you exactly the same benefits, or the same cover against risks. You will need to seek advice from someone who knows just what is available. The worst place to ask is the garage or dealer who sold you the car; almost certainly they are agents for one or two companies only. An insurance broker on the other hand earns his living from the commissions that insurance companies pay. He represents many firms and he will be able to offer unbiased advice. He will probably look after the formalities if you are unlucky enough to make a claim, so he will try to see that your policy is with a company noted for fair and swift settlements. If an insurance broker is too hard to find, then the policies sponsored by the motoring associations are good, not the cheapest or the best, but very good value for money.

Membership of a motoring association is one of the best bargains that you can ever hope to make in motoring. In England and Wales, both the Automobile Association and the Royal Automobile Club offer for a small annual subscription a wide range of facilities. Telephone boxes positioned on main roads, route planning for a long-distance trip, breakdown and get-you-home services are invaluable. Many a motorist has blessed his subscription when late at night he has run out of petrol, and a gallon of petrol has been delivered to the car to see him on his way.

Running Costs, Maintenance and Servicing
A log book contains details of the present and earlier owners of a car and a full description of the vehicle. Once a car has been bought, and the log book changed hands, then the expenses really begin. New car or second-hand, the moment that it is driven from the showroom or garage, depreciation begins.

Depreciation is the fall in value of a car. New cars lose 10 to 15 per cent immediately they are driven on the highway. Used cars drop more slowly in value, and a vehicle bought for £500 will probably lose £100 in a year. Partly this is due to the number of extra miles travelled, and also it is older. Some of the fall is the difference between the price a dealer will pay and the price he asks when selling to make a profit.

Running costs are divided into two parts. Maintenance and the actual fuel expenditure per mile. Petrol will be consumed faster in built up areas, where there is a great deal of traffic. Long distance journeys are more economical. An average figure for miles per gallon will soon give the cost of petrol over a mile. A rough estimate of oil consumption, and other expenses such as anti-freeze, will give a total running cost for each mile. Generally the more powerful the car, and the older it is, the higher these running costs will be.

Maintenance is a different matter entirely. Some people are gifted, they are born mechanics and with the aid of the hand-book they can carry out all running repairs, improvements and adjustments. Other drivers are completely helpless when confronted with a confusion of pipes, wires and strange looking objects. Garages are essential for them and manpower costs alone will soon send the bill soaring. There is a natural reaction to skimp on routine maintenance but this is false economy. Maintenance can prevent more expensive repairs that come round too often if the car is not looked after properly.

The Automobile Association keeps a large fleet of vehicles and their drivers are skilled mechanics. Schedules and practice are well worth copying. The private motorist will benefit if he can follow the full maintenance programme. Each day their drivers complete a daily servicing. Petrol and oil are checked, windows cleaned and the wipers are tested. Tyres are checked for pressure, cuts and uneven wear noted, and bits of flint and gravel are removed. Horn, lights and batteries are checked as being serviceable; water level in the battery, its connections and dynamo charging are noted. Clutch and brake reservoirs are checked and if the level is low the cause must be found.

With practice the complete procedure takes only ten minutes. It's easy enough—and as easy to ignore the schedule on a cold winter morning, already a little late for work.

Daily servicing only works when it is carried out regularly. Aircraft are only allowed to take off after a thorough servicing because engine failure or other damage in mid-air could be very dangerous. In a car, similar faults only cause inconvenience. Ten minutes a day is little enough to enjoy trouble-free motoring.

Period maintenance can be included on a schedule, from say every 3000 miles when the oil is changed up to 24,000 miles when a complete electrical overhaul is called for. Routine maintenance should take place each month, making an ideal time to replace brake linings, bleed hydraulic systems and change tyres. Manufacturers lay down their recommendations in their car handbooks. If you can follow these operations properly then you are fortunate. Should you rely upon a garage, then you must either trust them to do what is required, or arrange for some sort of supervision and check after each visit.

Running a car is not cheap. Even this catalogue of costs has ignored parking meters and garages, and the odd parking ticket. Reckless drivers may even find themselves in a police court, with fines to be included in the total price to pay for the pleasures of motoring.

THINGS TO DO

1 Compare the cost of servicing a car, with the charge made by your local garage for some typical item. Examples could be (a) treating a door for rust; (b) the full 12,000 miles servicing.

2 Estimate, using any used car price book manuals available to you, the cost of buying a three year old car of your choice, and selling it one year later.

3 Choose a model of car known to you. Imagine that it is three years old. Estimate the running costs for one year, including servicing, but without replacement. Assume it

starts off the year with 35,000 miles on the clock, and covers 12,000 miles more.

4 Estimate, for the three year old car of your choice, the cost of insurance. Look at different types of policies, and different companies. How does the cost of this insurance vary with age and experience?

5 Repeat questions 2, 3 and 4 with a new car. Suppose it covers 10,000 miles in the first year.

6 A car is essential. Discuss this statement for the area in which you live.

7 What are the advantages and disadvantages of owning a car?

8 There are more cars on the roads each year. What are some of the problems they bring, and how can they be solved?

9 What is the main difference between family life today, and before the invention of the motor car?

10 Manufacturers of cars for many years concentrated on making their models faster and more stylish. What are some of the safety measures that have been introduced into cars over the past ten or twenty years? How many of these safety measures are now enforced by law?

11 What are the advantages and disadvantages of hiring a car for (a) a two week holiday. (b) a full year? Compare these costs with the *true* costs of owning a car for a year.

Chapter Twelve   Spending for Pleasure

Spending for pleasure may mean that you have nothing to show for your money at the end except happy memories. Holidays are a good example. They are precious, lasting for only two or three weeks; they allow you to live a different type of life away from the normal working scene.

Your sort of holiday will probably be very different from the type your parents would choose. Brothers and sisters in the same family will rarely agree on where or when or even how a holiday should be spent.

Within Great Britain there is all the choice that anybody could reasonably need. Busy bustling holiday resorts on the coast, with crowded sands and dance halls, and your favourite food with chips at the boarding house. In complete contrast there are youth hostels in mountainous and hilly areas reached only after a ten mile hike. There are holidays on the water in cabin cruisers or canal boats; pony-trekking or mountaineering—the list is endless.

Holidays in Britain can be arranged quite simply. It takes only a letter or two to the resort where you want to stay, or perhaps to the holiday camp or outdoor centre. Full board makes eating simple—bed and breakfast means that you have more freedom over times and visits away—it will all be familiar fare. Travelling is easy: you can take the train or the cheaper express coach, your own car or that of a friend, there are few problems in this country.

Holidays abroad have become more and more popular in recent years. The British have found that there are places where the sun shines all day, guaranteed; this can never be said within our own island. Holidays can be arranged so that you can stay in a far away place, and eat British food, drink tea, talk English and never have to worry about anything foreign except the money. This is what some people want.

Others go abroad, partly for the sun, but mostly for the excitement of change. Other cultures, strange foods, different customs, and ways of living. A change is as good as a rest.

It is straightforward enough to plan your own holiday abroad. A travel agent will help you, selling air, boat and train tickets, and arranging a hotel. Except in the busiest capital cities of Europe hotels do not have to be booked in advance. In each town, near the railway station there will be a Town Bureau, that either provides the holidaymaker with lists of all the hotels and guest houses in the area, or arranges a booking there and then. This gives you the freedom to move on each day or to stay, as you please. Young people and those who love walking will probably try the youth hostels which enable you to live abroad for a few pounds each week. Comfort lovers have the choice of a friendly private house or the best hotel in town.

Package Holidays

Most travellers abroad do not bother to make their own plans. They visit their travel agent and take home brochures published by tour operators. Within these glossy, highly coloured pages will be hundreds of package holidays. Everything arranged from the outward flight, meals and hotel accommodation, to the journey home again. Such holidays are cheaper than the kind you can organise yourself, because the operator charters the aircraft, books the rooms, and administers all the service in bulk. Hotel and aircraft costs are particular bargains. If there is a tour going where you want, when you want, it will most certainly be value for money.

Brochures are designed to sell holidays. They present all the good points—and forget to mention the bad ones. If there is an omission, such as distance to the sea, then it is probably deliberate. 'Hotel coach provided to the town' can only mean that the site is so isolated that transport must be made available.

Package holiday prices vary considerably. Mostly you pay

for what you get. The more the holiday costs, the better the accommodation and the facilities provided. On the other hand an identical holiday offered by two different operators may vary by as much as £10. One firm is better at business, has arranged bargain terms at the hotel, and perhaps is content with a lower profit.

You must decide the country, hotel, and resort yourself. Some places will be busy, others very quiet. You choose according to your taste. Once this is done, read the conditions and small print details in a holiday brochure carefully. It is possible for an eight day holiday to be only six nights abroad, if you leave a little before midnight, and travel back in the small hours. It is worth checking that you are allowed to go straight to your room on arrival, and may stay there until just before you leave for home. Many a good holiday has been spoilt by the long wait for a 10 pm coach, after vacating a room at midday.

What should a holiday cost? It will almost certainly cost more than the price mentioned at the top of the page in the brochure. You may wish to spend longer at the resort, or travel in the busy season, and not at the very beginning or end of the summer period. Holiday prices will be affected by when you fly—weekend and day flights are much more expensive. How will you get to the airport? Most tours begin and end from there. Are you fussy about the type of room? Sea views, showers or bathrooms, staying in the main building rather than in a detached annexe, are all factors that add to the cost. Insurance is an absolute necessity, and to be worthwhile must cover illness before the date of leaving, with compensation for any lost deposits or cancellation charges. It should provide for any medical expenses that are incurred while on holiday with, if necessary, transport home again, loss of baggage and money, and the cost of an accident. This insurance is only expensive when you do not bother to take it out.

Holiday Costs

Let us look at a typical holiday advertised to Spain. At the top of the page it proudly proclaims sunshine holidays of one and two weeks at prices 'from £34'. In fact there are only three departure dates in the year when you can take the £34 holiday, and this is the price for eight days. The fifteen day holidays begin at £42, and this value is only available in April.

You decide that you would like to buy this package, but will be holidaying in July, and want to travel on Saturday by a day flight. The minimum price for the holiday is £42, and to this you must add £12 for the week-end day travel. The price quoted is for Thursday night travel only. It would have been only £5 more to travel by day on Wednesday. You are travelling to Spain in the High Season, which is the period when everybody wants to go—July to early September. There is an additional charge of £1 per night, or a total of £14. So far the holiday is costing £68 (£42 + £12 + £14).

This is not the end of the calculation. If you want a single room you will be charged another 25p for each day. A room with a bath costs 50p a day supplement, while the best rooms with bath, sea view and balcony are an extra £1.10 each day. For the best rooms the total cost of a 15 day holiday, airport to airport comes to £83.40. To this you must add the cost of getting to the airport and home again, insurance cover, and any taxes. This is a far cry from the £34 or even the basic £42 quoted. With spending money, this holiday will work out at over £100 if you want the best. Even now this holiday will be far cheaper than if you went out on a scheduled airline flight, and booked in at the same hotel yourself. Package holidays are a bargain, and with the large companies with proven reputations you will be well satisfied, getting value for money. You will never get something for nothing—the more you pay, the better the holiday.

Pleasure Spending
Spending for pleasure is a fair occupation after working hard for one's weekly wages. Life would be very dull if it was one long routine of saving and spending on the necessities of life. The margin between income and planned expenditure can go in many directions. It can disappear in smoke and drink, vanish in

a visit to the theatre, be consumed in an evening out—these are all perfectly reasonable ways of spending money.

Tastes vary. What would be an exciting evening for one could be boredom for another. Not everyone will share the taste of the Shakespeare enthusiast, the opera or ballet lover at the so-called ' heavy ' end of the cultural scale. An evening spent dancing, or at a pop concert, could be more popular, but this is not for everyone.

Pleasure and Investment

Spending for pleasure can be spending as an investment. It is amazing what people collect. If objects exist in quantity, they will be collected by someone somewhere. Beer and wine labels, butterflies and marbles, old magazines and gramophone records all have their addicts. Some collecting themes have a wider following. The more popular the topic, the greater the number of people who collect, then the more likely that prices will go up in time.

Take three different collecting areas. Paintings—and this means original paintings—are collected by the very rich. They seek the old masters, canvases created hundreds of years ago by the greatest artists, and they buy and sell them for anything up to and over a million pounds a time. These prices are for the very best—as judged by international standards of artistic taste. Even paintings by the second and third rate followers of the great will attract prices in the hundreds of pounds range. New paintings, modern paintings by artists that have yet to prove their skill, or at least have still to be recognised by the art loving public, will fetch but a few pounds. It is possible to buy an original painting for very little. Should you choose well, then perhaps it will fetch many times that amount in twenty years time, If not, it will be hard to get back the money you paid for it.

Paintings can be an investment. Although the expensive items are beyond most people's purses, it is quite reasonable to buy a picture that you like, for the pleasure it will give hanging on the wall of your living room. If you are lucky or talented, and have chosen well, it may be an investment too.

Another area is fine silver. Silver has an intrinsic value. You will never be able to buy it for less than its melted down value. As the years fly by, the price of an ounce of silver rises. In addition to this basic value, you will pay extra for the craftsmanship that has gone into the work. Because in some periods the workmanship was exceptionally fine, objects from these periods are sought after—you can expect to pay more for such pieces.

Silver, manufactured in Great Britain is hallmarked. This is a system of Government control, which stamps all pieces with the year in which they are sent for examination. The stamping is also proof that the silver content is pure. When buying British silver you can at least be sure that you are buying the true metal.

Silver can be cheap—silver teaspoons are often to be found for pence—or expensive. Georgian silver is wonderful, beautifully designed, and the more ornate table pieces and silver services fetch thousands upon thousands of pounds. Silver collecting can begin as a hobby. The pieces are a delight to the eye, and are bought for the aesthetic pleasure they give; in addition, they may increase in value making them a wise investment.

The third area where pleasure can also be investment is stamp collecting. Stamps are cheap enough—you can usually get them for nothing off old envelopes that come into the house. True enough, but they are so common that they have no value at all. Unused stamps may be worth more, but before anyone can buy stamps for investment they must know what they are doing. Some investors simply tell their dealer to spend say one thousand pounds on stamps and may never see them. This is investment, but hardly pleasure.

Stamp collecting, like any other hobby has its rules. You must know what to collect and what to throw out. You must learn how to look after the stamps, how to keep them safely, how to recognise the good from the bad, and the best place to buy stamps. This done, you can collect for pleasure.

A first collection is hardly likely to be an investment. Later with practice, having made mistakes on the way, you will recognise the good stamps, the best issues, the items in demand,

and if they are good sound copies, then over a long period of time they will advance in price as does any other commodity in demand.

Paintings, silver, stamps—these three are typical of the sort of things that can be collected for profit. They are as different from each other as they are from the many other things that prove that collecting can be a pleasure and an investment too.

THINGS TO DO

1 Arrange a holiday to either a south of Spain resort or to Yugoslavia. You wish to travel out on the first Saturday in August, and stay for fifteen days. compare the costs of going by air, and booking your own hotel, with those offered by tour operators.

2 Take an example from any large tour holiday operator's brochure, where there are holidays offered for at least six months of the year. Draw a chart showing the total cost for a fifteen day holiday in the best room, and for an eight day holiday in basic accommodation for the whole period.

3 Discuss why more and more people are taking holidays abroad. Should this be a source of worry to British holiday resorts?

4 Make a table of the ways to cross over to the European mainland by car. Compare the costs for a family of four, by these routes.

5 Plan a walking holiday through either the Lake District or the Scottish highlands or the North Wales National Park, staying at Youth Hostels.

6 Write about the sort of holiday that you would like to take.

7 Choose a subject for collecting. Read all you can about your choice. Where could you obtain examples for your collection? What are the investment possibilities?

8 Spending for pleasure covers many areas. List some of the possibilities that have not been covered here.

Appendix   Useful Contacts

While preparing my course and later when writing this book I have found the following organisations to be of particular assistance.

Banks

Bank Education Service: This service arranges visits by speakers and produces a wide range of publications. Contact the Secretary, Bank Education Service, 10 Lombard Street, London E.C.3.

Particularly helpful are the following leaflets:
The Life Story of a Cheque
A Selection of Facsimile Bank Forms and Documents
Study Booklet Series Nos. 1 to 12; immediately important are:
No. 1 The Role of the Banks
No. 2 How to Handle Cheques
No. 5 Borrowing from a Bank

Each of the clearing banks publishes numerous individual publications for customers' use and many of these are directly relevant. Your local bank manager will not only help but also will probably invite you to visit him and see behind the scenes at his branch. The National Giro publishes a useful Handbook containing a digest of that organisation's services.

Building Societies

The Building Societies Association, 14 Park Street, London W.1, publishes booklets with supplementary material.
Building Societies: Their history and work (teachers handbook)
Building Societies: What they are and what they do (for students)

1000 Years of Houses
10,000 Years of Money
All these booklets touch on points mentioned in this book, and in some cases develop topics further.

Most High Streets have a branch office of one or more building societies. These branches will be only too pleased to provide all the literature that one could wish for covering the various types of savings accounts.

Shopping

The Consumers Association, 14 Buckingham Street, London WC2N 6DS, is a non-profit making organisation concerned about the standards of goods and services. Their magazine *Which?* has a supplement *Money Which?* and they are both well worth the subscription.

In addition they have prepared a number of specialist books. The following are relevant in some degree, although they are very detailed and specific:
Owning a Car
The Law for Consumers
Buying Secondhand
The Law for Motorists
Insurance and the Consumer
The Legal Side of Buying a House

Inland Revenue

The local Inspector of Taxes will be able to supply copies of:
Income Tax: Paying Tax for the First Time
Income Tax: Personal Allowances

Life Assurance

The Life Offices' Association, Aldermary House, Queen Street, Cheapside, London E.C.4 and The Associated Scottish Life Offices, 23 St. Andrew Square, Edinburgh publish:
Life Assurance and You (very simple guide to policies)
Life Assurance: A Brief Outline of the Business (rather more technical)
How Life Assurance Works (the mechanics of assurance)

Money makes the Wheels Go Round (brief economic details)
How Life Assurance Works (A supplement produced by Educational Productions Limited on behalf of the Associations, to accompany three wall charts).

National Savings
Local Savings Committees and District Offices are listed in telephone directories. The following central organisations will put you in touch with your District Commissioner, who will arrange visits to schools either to discuss money management projects or to talk to students:
National Savings Committee London
National Savings Committee for Scotland, Edinburgh
Ulster Savings Committee, Belfast.
Investing in National Savings (Desk book for investment advisers)
Mathematics of Money (Handbook for teachers)
Money Matters (students' and teachers' editions)
Looking Ahead (Handbook on money management teaching)
Nine Ways to a Nest Egg (useful, brief give-away pamphlet)

Stock Exchange
Public Relations Officer, the Stock Exchange, London E.C.2
The following are available:
Wallchart and *The Stock Exchange—How it works* (teaching notes)
Wallchart and *A Company: How it is formed and financed* (teachers' notes)
    The following are give-away leaflets:
Visitors Gallery: The Stock Exchange London
The Jobbers Job
The Buying and Selling of Shares
A Career on the Stock Exchange
The Stock Exchange and You.
Copies of contract notes and transfer forms are also available.

Unit Trusts

Association of Unit Trust Managers, 306-308 Salisbury House, Finsbury Circus, London E.C.2.

Directory of Unit Trusts (statistical details of unit trusts managed by members of the Association).

Index

Annual General Meeting, 97
Annuity, 79
Assurance, Life, *see* life assurance

Bank charges, 40, 46
Bank Education Service, 150
Bank giro, 38
Bank of England, 39
Bank rate, 26
Bank, commercial, 26, 34
  National Savings, 20
  savings, 26
  services of, 41
  Trustee Savings, 23
Bankers guarantee card, 41
Banking, 34
Barclaycard, 73
Barter, 9
Bonds, premium, 24
Bonds, savings, 25
British Savings Bonds, 25
Budget, 11
Budget accounts, 69
Budget, council, 117
Budget, national, 105
Building societies, 27, 54
  history of, 27
Building societies Association, 150
Buying a house, 52

Buying money, 68

Car, buying a, 135
Car insurance, 137
Car maintenance, 139
Cheque, 34
  crossed, 35
  giro, 44
  open, 35
  travellers, 42
Commercial savings, 31
Consumers Association, 151
Contract note, 96
Contract of employment, 17
Cooperative Bank, 43
Cooperative Societies, 31, 128
Council savings, 31
Council, local, 117
Credit, 66, 137
Credit card, 72
Credit sale, 68
Credit transfer, *see* bank giro
Credit without charge, 70
Current account, 35

Debentures, 92
Department stores, 128
Deposit accounts, 26, 29
Dodson, James, 80
Dowdeswell, William, 23
Drawer of cheque, 36

Endowment assurance, 79
Ernie, 24
Estate Agents, 51
Estate duty, 112
Exchange, 10
Executor service, 42

Gilt edged, 92
Giro, National, 25, 43
   cheques, 44
   documents, 45
   envelopes, 44
   identity card, 48
   procedure, 46
   transfer, 44
Government, local, 117
   national, 105
   stocks, 26
Guarantee, 130
Guarantee card, 41

Hire purchase, 31, 67
Hiring, 75
Holiday costs, 145
   in Britain, 143
   package, 144
Home shopping, 70
House contract, 53
   searching for a, 51

Inflation, 10
Inspector of Taxes, 151
Insurance, 59
   car, 137
   contents, 61
   holiday, 63, 145
   home, 59
   National, 11, 16, 112

personal liability, 62
   weather, 64
Insurance broker, 63
Investment account, 22
Investment trust, 100
Investment for pleasure, 147

Jobbers, 92

Life assurance, 31, 78
   annuity, 79
   endowment, 79
   history, 78
   policies, 82
   term assurance, 79
   whole life, 79
Life Offices Association, 151
Loans, 93
Local government, 117

Medium of exchange, 9
Money, 9
Moneylenders, 76
Money management, 10
Monthly account, 71
Mortgage, 56
Multiple stores, 128

National budget, 105
National giro, see giro
National Health Service, 113
National Insurance, 112
National Savings, 20, 107, 152
   banks, 20
   investment accounts, 22
   ordinary accounts, 22
   bonds, 25
   certificates, 23
   premium bonds, 24

save-as-you-earn, 25
stamps, 25
stocks, 26

Ordinary accounts, 22
Ordinary shares, 93
Overdrafts, 68

Pawnbrokers, 76
PAYE, 12, 110
Paying in slips, 38
Pension, 16, 113
Perquisites, 18
Personal budget, 11
Personal expenses, 13
Personal income, 13
Personal liability, 62
Personal loan, 69
Pleasure spending, 143
Policy, 59, 82
Post Office Savings Bank, 20
Preference shares, 93
Premium, 60
Premium bonds, 24
Profits, life assurance, 86
Proposal form, 60

Rates, 119
Rates calculations, 122
References, 36
Regular Savings account, 29
Retirement, 113
Revolving credit, 69
Running a car, 135

Salary, 10, 14
Sales of Goods Act, 126
Save-as-you-earn, 25, 31

Savings, 14
account, 27, 29
Bank, 20, 23
bonds, 25
certificates, 23
commercial, 31
National, 20
Save-as-you-earn, 25
schemes, 102
stamps, 25
Securities, 91
Servicing, 131
Shares, 91
bonus, 98
buying, 95
choice, 99
commission, 97
dividends, 97
nominal value, 97
price, 94
rights, 98
selling, 99
split, 98
warrants, 97
Share account, 29
Shopping, 126
Shopping hints, 129
Shopping rights, 126
Sickness benefit, 17
Standing order, 38, 48
Statement, bank, 39
Stockbroker, 92
Stock Exchange, 91, 152
Stocks, 91
Government, 26
Social Security, 17, 113
Solicitor, 54
Superannuation, 17
Surveyors, 54

Tax, income, 42, 107, 109
Taxation, 107, 108
Taxes, 111
Term assurance, 79
Third party cover, 138
Trade Descriptions Act, 126
Trading Checks, 70
Transfers, giro, 44
Travellers' cheques, 42

Trust, investment, 100
Trust, unit, 101
Trustee Savings Bank, 23

Unit Trust, 101, 153

Wages, 10, 14
Whole life assurance, 79
Working conditions, 16